ORGANIZED LIVING WITH ADHD MADE SIMPLE

EASY STRATEGIES TO TRANSFORM CHAOS INTO CALM, DECLUTTER YOUR MIND, DEFEAT DISTRACTION, AND OVERWHELM TO UNLOCK YOUR FULL POTENTIAL

NIKKII RAMIREZ

© **Copyright Nikkii Ramirez 2024 - All rights reserved.**

The content within this book may not be reproduced, duplicated or transmitted without direct written permission from the author or the publisher.

Under no circumstances will any blame or legal responsibility be held against the publisher, or author, for any damages, reparation, or monetary loss due to the information contained within this book. Either directly or indirectly. You are responsible for your own choices, actions, and results.

Legal Notice:

This book is copyright protected. This book is only for personal use. You cannot amend, distribute, sell, use, quote or paraphrase any part, of the content within this book, without the consent of the author or publisher.

Disclaimer Notice:

Please note the information contained within this document is for educational and entertainment purposes only. All effort has been expended to present accurate, up-to-date, reliable, complete information. No warranties of any kind are declared or implied. Readers acknowledge that the author is not engaging in the rendering of legal, financial, medical or professional advice. The content within this book has been derived from various sources. Please consult a licensed professional before attempting any techniques outlined in this book.

By reading this document, the reader agrees that under no circumstances is the author responsible for any losses, direct or indirect, which are incurred as a result of the use of the information contained within this document, including, but not limited to, — errors, omissions, or inaccuracies.

CONTENTS

Introduction	5
1. Understanding ADHD and Its Impact on Organization	9
2. Getting Started: Mindset and Motivation	21
3. Time Management Techniques for ADHD	31
4. Room-by-Room Decluttering Strategies	41
5. Organizing Personal Spaces	51
6. Digital Decluttering	61
7. Maintenance and Habits	73
8. Emotional and Mental Well-being	83
9. Tools and Resources	93
10. Involving Family and Friends	103
11. Special Circumstances	115
12. Cultivating a Long-Term Organized Life	125
Conclusion	135
References	139

INTRODUCTION

You wake up in the morning, your alarm blaring, and the first thing you see is the pile of laundry you forgot to fold last night. You stumble to the kitchen, stepping over shoes you meant to put away, only to find a sink full of dishes staring back at you. Your phone buzzes with notifications, reminding you of tasks you're already behind. Sound familiar?

For adults with ADHD, this isn't just a rough morning—it's a daily battle. The relentless chaos and disorganization can make it feel like you're always playing catch-up. It's more than just an inconvenience; it's a constant source of stress and frustration that impacts your productivity and quality of life.

But what if I told you there's a way to turn this chaos into calm? What if you could wake up to a tidy room, a clean kitchen, and a clear mind? Organized living can be a game-changer. This book is here to show you how to achieve that. We'll tackle the clutter, the distractions, and the overwhelm with simple, easy-to-follow strategies. You'll learn how to declutter both your physical space and your mind, paving the way for a more intentional and stress-free life.

Who am I to guide you on this journey? My name is Nikkii Ramirez, and I have spent years helping adults with ADHD navigate the challenges of everyday life. I've walked in your shoes, faced the same struggles, and found ways to overcome them. My background and my years of experience working with individuals with ADHD have equipped me with the tools and insights to make a real difference. I'm passionate about sharing what I've learned and helping you achieve the organized, intentional life you deserve.

So, what can you expect from this book? First, we'll dive into time management techniques tailored to ADHD brains. You'll discover room-by-room decluttering strategies that make the process less daunting. We'll also explore digital decluttering because, let's face it, our devices can be just as cluttered as our homes. Finally, we'll discuss how to maintain your new, organized lifestyle so that you don't fall back into old habits.

The benefits of organized living are immense. You'll reduce stress and free up mental space to focus on what truly matters. You'll gain more free time to enjoy hobbies, spend with loved ones, or simply relax. Most importantly, you'll create a peaceful, productive environment that supports your well-being.

I remember working with a client named Sarah, who struggled with keeping her home in order. Every day felt like a race against the clock, and she was always exhausted. We started with small steps—just organizing her desk, then her kitchen. Slowly but surely, she began to see changes. Her home became a sanctuary rather than a source of stress. She even found time to pick up painting, a hobby she had abandoned years ago. Sarah's transformation was inspiring, and it reinforced my belief that organized living is attainable for everyone, including you.

Now, it's your turn. This book is your guide, your roadmap to a more organized, intentional life. Each chapter will provide you with actionable steps and positive affirmations to keep you motivated. You don't have to tackle everything at once. Start small, be patient with yourself, and celebrate each victory, no matter how tiny.

Ready to take the first step? Let's transform that chaos into calm together. Dive into the chapters ahead, armed with the knowledge that change is not only possible but also incredibly rewarding. You deserve a life that is less about managing clutter and more about enjoying the moments that truly matter.

Key Takeaway: This book is a sympathetic, step-by-step guide designed specifically for adults with ADHD. It aims to transform chaos into calm, enabling you to live a more intentional, stress-free life.

Let's get started. Your journey to organized living begins now.

I
UNDERSTANDING ADHD AND ITS IMPACT ON ORGANIZATION

You know those days when you can't seem to find your keys, your phone, or even your other shoe? Everything feels like it's hiding, and you end up late to work, frazzled before you even start your day. For adults with ADHD, these chaotic mornings aren't just occasional hiccups—they're a regular occurrence. The scattered piles of paperwork, the half-finished projects, and the perpetual search for lost items can make life feel like an endless game of hide and seek. But it's not just about the mess; it's about how this disorganization wreaks havoc on your mind and emotions.

This chapter dives into understanding why these struggles happen. It's not just because you're lazy or forgetful. It's about how ADHD affects your brain, particularly something called executive dysfunction. We'll break down what executive dysfunction is and how it impacts your ability to manage tasks, prioritize, and stay focused. By the end of this chapter, you'll have a clearer picture of why things get so chaotic and, more importantly, what you can do about it.

THE ADHD BRAIN: UNDERSTANDING EXECUTIVE DYSFUNCTION

Executive dysfunction is a fancy term for the brain's struggle to control thoughts, emotions, and actions. Think of it as the CEO of your brain going on an extended lunch break, leaving everything in disarray. The prefrontal cortex, located right behind your forehead, is primarily responsible for these executive functions. It's like the control tower at an airport, managing everything from flight plans to emergency landings. When it's not working correctly, planes (or in this case, tasks) get delayed, rerouted, or crash altogether.

This dysfunction affects your ability to plan, prioritize, and execute tasks. Imagine trying to cook a complex meal without a recipe. You start boiling water but forget to chop the vegetables. You then realize you don't have all the ingredients. It's frustrating and disorganized. In daily life, this might mean you struggle to start tasks, follow through on plans, or keep track of essential items. Your brain is like a computer with too many tabs open, making it hard to focus on any one thing.

The variability of executive dysfunction among individuals with ADHD is significant. Some people might find it mildly annoying, while for others, it's completely debilitating. Co-existing conditions like anxiety can exacerbate the symptoms, making it even harder to manage daily tasks. A friend of mine, Emily, used to describe her experience with executive dysfunction as trying to herd cats while juggling flaming torches. It's a vivid image, but it captures perfectly the chaos she felt in her mind.

Common ADHD behaviors like procrastination, impulsivity, forgetfulness, and disorganization are all linked to executive dysfunction. Procrastination isn't just putting things off; it's a result of your brain having trouble breaking tasks into smaller, manageable steps. Impulsivity can lead to starting new projects before finishing old ones, creating a whirlwind of half-done tasks. Forgetfulness isn't just about misplaced keys; it's your brain's way of struggling to hold on to information when it's overloaded. Disorganization stems from the difficulty in setting up and maintaining systems that keep life in order.

Let's break this down further with some examples. Difficulty starting tasks is a hallmark of executive dysfunction. You know you need to clean the kitchen, but the thought of where to start is paralyzing. Should you do the dishes first? Wipe the counters? The indecision keeps you stuck. Inability to follow through on plans is another issue. You might begin organizing your closet but get distracted halfway through by an old photo album you find, turning a simple task into a trip down memory lane.

Trouble keeping track of important items is also common. Your life feels like a never-ending scavenger hunt. Where did you put that bill you need to pay? What happened to the grocery list? It's not that you don't care; it's that your brain struggles to manage and store these details effectively.

The impact of executive dysfunction varies, but one thing is clear: it makes life more challenging. Understanding this can help you develop strategies to manage these difficulties. You're not alone in this, and knowing the why behind your struggles is the first step in finding solutions that work for you.

THE SCIENCE BEHIND ADHD: HOW IT AFFECTS YOUR DAILY LIFE

Ever wonder why your brain feels like it's on a never-ending rollercoaster? It all boils down to brain chemistry. Two main players in this chaotic ride are dopamine and norepinephrine. Think of dopamine as the brain's motivational speaker. It keeps you interested and engaged. Conversely, Norepinephrine is like the brain's alert system, keeping you focused and ready. In the ADHD brain, both of these neurotransmitters don't quite perform their duties as they should. This leads to problems with attention, focus, and impulse control. The prefrontal cortex, which is responsible for planning and decision-making, doesn't get enough of these neurotransmitters, making it harder to manage everyday tasks. Imagine trying to run a marathon with one shoe missing—it's not impossible, but it sure makes things a lot harder.

The functional differences in the ADHD brain are fascinating. For starters, the prefrontal cortex is often less active. This area is crucial for executive functions like planning, decision-making, and impulse control. When it's not firing on all cylinders, the result is a brain that's constantly struggling to keep up with the demands of daily life. This is why even simple tasks can feel overwhelming. Your brain is working overtime to compensate for these deficits, leaving you feeling exhausted and frustrated.

Let's talk about how these neurological quirks wreak havoc on daily routines. Take mornings, for example. For most people, getting ready involves a series of steps—wake up, shower, get dressed, eat breakfast, and head out the door. For someone with ADHD, each of these steps can feel like climbing a mountain. You might start getting dressed but get distracted by a text message. Next thing you know, you're scrolling through social media, and suddenly, you're running late. Managing work or school tasks is equally challenging. You sit down to start a project, but your mind keeps wandering to other things you need to do. By the end of the day, you've started ten different tasks but completed none.

Decision-making and prioritizing tasks can feel like trying to solve a Rubik's Cube blindfolded. You may struggle to weigh the pros and cons of a decision, leading to chronic indecisiveness. Setting realistic goals becomes a Herculean task because your brain finds it difficult to break down big projects into smaller, manageable steps. Instead, you either set the bar too high and get overwhelmed or set it too low and feel unaccomplished. This difficulty in prioritizing often means that urgent tasks get pushed aside for less important ones, creating a backlog that increases stress.

Speaking of stress, let's not forget how ADHD impacts emotional regulation. Many adults with ADHD are emotionally sensitive, feeling things more intensely than others. This heightened sensitivity can turn minor setbacks into major crises. The constant battle with disorganization adds fuel to the fire, making you feel like you're always on edge. Increased stress and anxiety from trying to keep everything in order can lead to emotional burnout. You might find yourself snapping at loved ones or feeling a sense of despair because it seems like you're always one step behind.

Imagine you've had a tough day at work—you're already frazzled, and then you come home to a sink full of dirty dishes and a living room that looks like a tornado hit it. The sight alone can trigger a stress response, making it difficult to unwind. This is the emotional toll of living with ADHD. Your environment directly impacts your mental state, and when that environment is chaotic, it's challenging to find peace.

Understanding the science behind ADHD can be eye-opening. It's not just about being easily distracted or forgetful. There's a complex interplay of brain chemistry and structure that influences every aspect of your life. Knowing this can be empowering. It's not your fault that your brain works this way, but knowing why it does can help you find strategies that work for you.

COMMON ORGANIZATIONAL CHALLENGES FACED BY ADULTS WITH ADHD

It's a typical Saturday morning, and you've decided today is the day you'll finally tackle the clutter. But as you look around, you feel paralyzed by the sheer volume of stuff. Piles of unopened mail, random knick-knacks, clothes draped over furniture, and a kitchen counter buried under a mountain of papers. This clutter accumulation isn't just an aesthetic issue; it's a daily obstacle course that drains your energy and focus. For adults with ADHD, clutter can accumulate at an alarming rate, turning your living space into a constant source of stress.

But clutter isn't the only challenge. Inconsistent cleaning and maintenance routines are another common hurdle. You might start with the best intentions—cleaning the bathroom and organizing the pantry—but keeping up with these routines is different. One week you're on top of everything, and the next, you're back to square one. This inconsistency makes it difficult to maintain an organized space, leading to a cycle of cleaning frenzies followed by periods of neglect.

Disorganized workspaces are a prime example of how these challenges manifest in daily life. Imagine sitting down at your desk, ready to tackle your to-do list, only to be greeted by a chaotic mess. Papers are scattered everywhere, pens are missing, and your computer screen is cluttered with open tabs. This disarray doesn't just slow you down; it sabotages your productivity. You spend more time searching for what you need than actually getting things done. Misplacing important documents or items, like your keys or that crucial report for work, adds another layer of frustration. It's not just inconvenient; it can have real consequences for your job and personal life.

Time perception is another intriguing aspect of ADHD that complicates organization. People with ADHD often have a distorted sense of time, known as "time blindness." You might underestimate how long a task will take, leading to rushed, incomplete, or abandoned efforts. For instance, you might think you can clean the whole house in an hour, only to find you've barely made a dent. This misjudgment makes it difficult to adhere to schedules, making you late for appointments or missing deadlines entirely.

These challenges don't exist in isolation; they compound each other, creating a perfect storm of disorganization. Clutter leads to increased stress, making it harder to focus and get things done. This stress can trigger procrastination, where you put off tasks because they seem too overwhelming to start. Procrastination then leads to guilt, as you berate yourself for not being more productive. It's a vicious cycle that can feel impossible to break.

Take the example of trying to organize your closet. You start by pulling everything out, intending to sort through each item. But halfway through, you get distracted by a box of old photos. Suddenly, you're reminiscing instead of organizing. Hours go by, and now you're left with an even bigger mess. This scenario is all too familiar for adults with ADHD. It's not just about lacking organizational skills; it's about the brain's difficulty staying focused on a single task.

Inconsistent routines also play a significant role. One week, you're on top of everything—your home is spotless, your bills are paid, and you even managed to cook a few meals. But the next week, life gets in the way. Maybe work was extra stressful, or you had a few social engagements. Suddenly, the cleaning and maintenance routines fall by the wayside, and you're back to living in chaos.

The compounding effects of these organizational challenges can be overwhelming. Clutter isn't just about physical space; it also affects your mental space. Walking into a cluttered room can instantly elevate your stress levels, making it difficult to relax or concentrate. This stress can lead to procrastination, where you delay tasks because they seem too daunting to tackle. Procrastination then leads to guilt, as you feel bad for not being more productive. It's a self-perpetuating cycle that can be challenging to escape.

Understanding these common organizational challenges is the first step toward finding solutions for you. Whether tackling clutter, establishing consistent routines, or managing time perception, recognizing the unique ways ADHD affects organization can help you develop strategies to overcome these hurdles. It's not about achieving perfection; it's about finding what works for you and making small, sustainable changes that improve your quality of life.

EMOTIONAL OVERWHELM AND ADHD: BREAKING THE CYCLE

Imagine walking into a room that looks like a tornado passed through it—clothes strewn everywhere, papers piled high, and random objects cluttering every surface. Now, imagine that's your life every single day. This isn't just an inconvenience; it's a trigger for emotional overwhelm. Clutter and chaos can make you feel trapped, raising your anxiety levels and making it difficult to breathe, let alone think clearly. The constant visual reminders of disorganization can amplify feelings of inadequacy and shame. You start to believe that you can't get it together, that you're failing at life in some fundamental way. This emotional weight can be paralyzing, making it even harder to take the first step toward cleaning up.

Increased anxiety and stress are common companions to a cluttered environment. The mess signals to your brain that there are unresolved tasks, creating a background hum of stress that never quite disappears. This can lead to heightened anxiety, making you feel on edge and irritable. The physical clutter translates into mental clutter, making it challenging to focus on anything else. Even simple tasks become overwhelming when your brain is constantly bombarded with visual stimuli reminding you of everything that needs to be done.

Feelings of shame and inadequacy often accompany this stress. You might look at your disorganized home and feel a deep sense of failure. Why can't you keep it together like everyone else seems to? This shame can be crippling, leading to a cycle of avoidance and procrastination. The more you avoid tackling the clutter, the worse it gets and the worse you feel. It's a vicious cycle that feeds on itself, making it impossible to break free.

But here's the good news: you can manage these emotional responses with practical strategies. Mindfulness and grounding exercises can be beneficial. Simple techniques like deep breathing, focusing on the present moment, or even a quick walk can help reduce anxiety and bring your mind back to a calmer state. These exercises act like a mental reset button, allowing you to approach tasks with a clearer, more relaxed mindset.

Cognitive-behavioral strategies can also make a big difference. This involves recognizing and challenging the negative thoughts that contribute to your feelings of overwhelm. For example, if you think, "I'll never get this place clean," challenge that thought by reminding yourself that you've tackled big tasks before. Breaking tasks into smaller, manageable steps can also help. Instead of thinking about cleaning the entire house, focus on one room, one corner, or even one drawer at a time. This makes the task less daunting and gives you a sense of accomplishment as you complete each small step.

Setting realistic and achievable goals is another crucial step. It's easy to get overwhelmed when your goals are too ambitious. Start small. Maybe today, your goal is to clear off the kitchen counter. Tomorrow, you can tackle the dining table. By setting small, manageable goals, you create a sense of momentum. Each small victory builds your confidence and makes it easier to keep going.

Self-compassion and patience are essential. It's so important to be kind to yourself during this process. Understand that progress takes time and that it's okay to have setbacks. Celebrate your small victories, no matter how insignificant they might seem. Did you manage to sort through that stack of mail? That's a win. Did you clear off your desk? Another win. These small accomplishments add up and help build your confidence.

I remember a time when I felt completely overwhelmed by the chaos in my own home. I started with just one small task —clearing off my nightstand. It seemed trivial, but completing that one small task gave me a sense of control and accomplishment. From there, I moved on to the next small task and then the next. Each step made the larger goal feel more achievable.

If you struggle with emotional overwhelm, start with small, manageable tasks. Set realistic goals and remember to be kind to yourself. Celebrate your progress, no matter how small. Understand that this is a journey, not a race. With patience and persistence, you can break the cycle of overwhelm and create a more organized, peaceful environment. It's about making progress, not achieving perfection. You've got this.

2
GETTING STARTED: MINDSET AND MOTIVATION

Picture this: It's a sunny Saturday afternoon, and you're surrounded by boxes, bags, and items that seem to have multiplied in your home overnight. You want to start organizing, but the sheer volume of stuff makes you want to crawl back into bed and pretend it doesn't exist. Sound familiar? Don't worry; you're not alone. Many of us have that one closet or drawer that seems to defy the laws of physics, constantly overflowing, no matter how often we try to tame it. But here's a little secret: starting with realistic goals can turn that overwhelming mountain of clutter into manageable molehills.

Setting achievable goals is crucial when you're facing a cluttered space. It's like planning a road trip; you wouldn't just hop in the car and drive without a map, right? The same goes for decluttering. Realistic goals act as your roadmap, guiding you step-by-step so you don't veer off course. They help avoid that dreaded feeling of overwhelm by breaking tasks into smaller, more digestible pieces. By focusing on one small area at a time, you can celebrate each tiny victory, building momentum that keeps you motivated to continue. It's the difference between saying, "I'm going to clean the entire house today," and "I'll organize one kitchen drawer before lunch."

To help you set these goals, let's dive into the SMART framework. SMART stands for Specific, Measurable, Achievable, Relevant, and Time-bound. Think of it as your trusty GPS for decluttering. Specific goals mean defining clear objectives, like targeting that pesky junk drawer instead of vaguely deciding to "get organized." Measurable criteria allow you to track progress—perhaps by counting the number of items you've discarded. Achievable goals are realistic; no need to aim for a magazine-worthy home overnight. Relevant goals should align with your broader vision, like creating a peaceful space for family dinners if that's important to you. Lastly, Time-bound goals keep you on track with deadlines, so you're not stuck in a never-ending cycle of "I'll do it tomorrow."

For example, instead of declaring war on your entire kitchen, set a goal to declutter one drawer per day. Or, aim to organize your home office by the end of the month. These realistic, SMART goals make the process feel less like a marathon and more like a series of short sprints. Remember, each drawer you tackle and each surface you clear is a step closer to the organized life you envision.

But life, as we know it, loves to throw curveballs. That's why flexibility is your new best friend. Maybe you planned to sort through old clothes, but a surprise deadline at work eats up your time. It's okay to adjust your goals. Recognizing and addressing unexpected obstacles without feeling discouraged is key. It's about progress, not perfection. Modify your plan as needed and keep moving forward. If you take a detour, remember that it's just part of the journey, not the end of the road.

So next time you feel the itch to declutter, grab a notepad and set a few SMART goals. Break those daunting tasks into smaller steps, and don't forget to pat yourself on the back for each little victory. You've got this—one drawer, one shelf, one room at a time. And when in doubt, remember that even the longest road trip starts with a single mile.

FINDING YOUR "WHY": THE EMOTIONAL AND PRACTICAL BENEFITS OF ORGANIZATION

Imagine standing in a room that feels like closing in on you, with clutter everywhere and no clear path to walk. It's more than just an untidy space; it reflects the chaos in your mind. Understanding why you want to organize goes beyond the superficial desire for a Pinterest-worthy home. It's about digging deeper, into motivations that drive you to declutter and organize. This isn't just a chore; it's a lifestyle shift. When you tap into your "why," you're not just cleaning up; you're reclaiming peace of mind. The emotional benefits are immense—reduced stress, less anxiety, and the sheer relief of a space that doesn't scream chaos. Picture waking up, and the first thing you see is a serene, tidy room. It's like a breath of fresh air, offering a sense of calm that sets a positive tone for your day. On a practical level, organization boosts productivity and efficiency. You'll spend less time searching for that elusive set of keys and more time focusing on what genuinely matters.

To find your "why," start by reflecting on your experiences with clutter. Remember when you missed an important deadline because you couldn't find the needed paperwork? Or how about when you felt completely overwhelmed by the mess in your closet, only for it to trigger an unnecessary shopping spree? Reflecting on these experiences can help you pinpoint the triggers and consequences of disorganization. Then, visualize your ideal organized life. Picture how it feels to walk into a home where everything has its place. Imagine the satisfaction of knowing exactly where to find your favorite book or the peace of seeing a clean kitchen counter. Use this visualization as your guiding light, a reminder of what you're working towards.

Organization doesn't just impact your physical space; it can transform various aspects of your life. A harmonious home environment can improve relationships—no more arguments over misplaced items or the stress of last-minute cleaning before guests arrive. Instead, you'll create a space where everyone feels at ease, fostering better communication and connection. At work or during hobbies, mental clarity, and focus become more accessible when your surroundings aren't a distraction. You'll find it easier to concentrate, allowing your creativity and productivity to flourish.

Let me share a story about a friend named Lisa. As a busy professional, she juggled work, family, and personal commitments. Her home reflected her hectic life, with piles of papers and clothes scattered everywhere. She finally decided enough was enough. By organizing her house, she found a new sense of balance. Her mornings became less frantic, her evenings more relaxing. She even discovered time for yoga, something she had always wanted to try. For Lisa, organization wasn't just about tidying up; it was a catalyst for positive change.

Then there's Mark, a parent who struggled with the chaos of raising kids. Toys were forever underfoot, and finding a clean surface to eat on was like a treasure hunt. Mark decided to involve the whole family in the organizing process, turning it into a fun bonding activity. Slowly, their home transformed into a peaceful haven. The kids knew where their toys belonged, reducing daily stress and making cleanup a breeze. The organization brought order and a newfound peace that benefited the entire family.

These stories highlight the transformative power of organization. It's not just about creating a tidy space; it's about improving your quality of life. Whether it's finding time for self-care, fostering better relationships, or simply enjoying a clutter-free environment, the benefits are manifold. So, what's your "why"? Take a moment to ponder this question and let it guide your organizing efforts. Your "why" is the compass that will navigate you through the clutter, leading you to a more intentional and fulfilling life.

OVERCOMING FEAR OF FAILURE: EMBRACING IMPERFECTION

It's a feeling many know all too well: the nagging voice in your head that whispers, "What if you fail?" This fear of failure can be a persistent companion, especially when you've attempted to organize your space before and ended up back where you started. It's like trying to diet with a freezer full of ice cream—tempting to start, easy to slip up. And let's not forget the perfectionism trap that lures you in with promises of immaculate spaces and perfectly labeled storage bins. Perfectionism can be the enemy of progress, leaving you stuck in a cycle of inaction. You might think, "If I can't do it perfectly, why bother?"

But what if we flipped the script? What if, instead of aiming for flawlessness, we focused on progress—no matter how small? Embracing imperfection doesn't mean settling for mediocrity; recognizing that any step forward is a win. It's about making small, incremental changes and understanding that setbacks are part of the process. Rome wasn't built in a day, and neither is an organized home. So let's shift that mindset. Think of each small change as a building block, creating a foundation for larger success. And when you encounter bumps in the road, remember they're just that—bumps, not dead ends.

Now, let's talk about practical ways to overcome the fear that holds you back. Start with low-stakes, achievable tasks to build confidence. Tackle that elusive sock drawer or organize your bookshelf. These tasks serve as warm-ups, easing you into the bigger challenges. As you complete each task, practice self-compassion and positive self-talk. Instead of berating yourself for what you haven't done, celebrate what you have. Say to yourself, "I've made progress today," and mean it. This isn't just about organizing your home; it's about changing the narrative in your head.

Consider the story of John, another friend of mine and a confessed perfectionist who struggled with fear of failure. Each time he tried to organize his garage, he became overwhelmed by the need for it to be perfect. But once he started focusing on progress rather than perfection, things changed. He began with small tasks, like sorting through old tools. Gradually, his confidence grew. He realized that his garage didn't need to look like a showroom to be functional. As he let go of perfectionism, he found joy in the process, not just the outcome.

Then there's Maria, who faced the daunting task of organizing her overflowing kitchen pantry. The thought made her cringe, fearing she'd just mess it up again. But Maria decided to embrace imperfection. She tackled one shelf at a time, celebrating each completed section with a small reward —a cup of her favorite coffee. This small shift in mindset gave her the courage to keep going. Her pantry might not have made it to the cover of a magazine, but it was organized enough for her to find what she needed. And that was more than enough.

Embracing imperfection means permitting yourself to be human. It's about understanding that it's okay not to be perfect and that everyone stumbles. The key is to get back up and keep going. By setting realistic expectations and focusing on progress, you can overcome the fear of failure and achieve a sense of accomplishment that motivates you to continue. Remember, even the smallest step forward is in the right direction.

BUILDING MOMENTUM: QUICK WINS TO BOOST YOUR CONFIDENCE

Have you ever tackled a project that just seemed too big to finish? Maybe, just like John, you started organizing your garage, only to find yourself surrounded by half-empty boxes and forgotten gadgets, wondering where to begin. That's where the beauty of quick wins comes into play. They're like little shots of adrenaline for your motivation. Achieving small, immediate successes can do wonders for your confidence and drive. There's a psychological boost that comes from these quick wins. They offer a tangible sense of accomplishment, like crossing a finish line you didn't even know existed. You begin to see the fruits of your labor, and suddenly, the mammoth task of organizing your entire home doesn't seem so unachievable now.

So what does a quick win look like? Imagine opening that notorious junk drawer in your kitchen—the one where batteries, pens, and random screws go to hide. Spend ten minutes sorting it out. Or maybe you take a few moments to tidy up the entryway, clearing shoes and bags to make it welcoming again. Perhaps you choose to declutter a small section of your closet, throwing out those old t-shirts you've meant to let go of. These small, manageable tasks can be completed quickly, yet they make a significant difference. Each of these quick wins is an opportunity to pat yourself on the back and say, "I did it!"

GETTING STARTED: MINDSET AND MOTIVATION • 29

Now, how do you make these quick wins a regular part of your routine? The key is to integrate them into your daily life without feeling like they're yet another chore on your endless list. Try setting aside 10 to 15 minutes daily for a quick decluttering session. Think of it like a coffee break but with the added benefit of a tidier home. You can even create a checklist to track your completed wins. There's something incredibly satisfying about checking off tasks, no matter how small. Over time, these quick wins can become a habit, a daily ritual that brings you closer to a more organized space.

The cumulative impact of these quick wins is where the magic truly happens. It's not just about the immediate boost you get from completing a task. It's about building a daily decluttering habit, which gradually transforms larger areas through consistent effort. Like drops filling a bucket, each small success adds up, leading to a significant change over time. Before you know it, those little wins have combined to create a more organized and peaceful environment. You'll find that areas of your home that once felt chaotic and overwhelming are now manageable and inviting.

These quick wins aren't just about tidying up your space and shifting your mindset. They teach you that progress is possible, even when you seem surrounded by chaos. They show you that you don't have to wait for the perfect moment or a free weekend to organize. You can make meaningful changes in small, consistent steps. And in doing so, you create a ripple effect that impacts other areas of your life, boosting your confidence and motivation in ways you never expected.

As we wrap up this chapter, remember that quick wins are your secret weapon in the fight against clutter. They're the small victories that lead to significant changes. By incorporating them into your routine, you'll build momentum and gain confidence with each step. Next, we'll explore how to tackle time management, giving you more tools to create the organized, intentional life you strive for.

3

TIME MANAGEMENT TECHNIQUES FOR ADHD

You know those days when your to-do list seems to have a mind of its own? It starts with a few tasks, but by the time you're halfway through your morning coffee, the list has mysteriously multiplied, like rabbits in a hat trick. The anxiety of not knowing where to start, coupled with the fear of dropping the ball, can leave you feeling like you're stuck in quicksand. But here's a little secret: time management doesn't have to be a mythical beast. It's all about finding techniques that work with your ADHD, not against it.

THE POMODORO TECHNIQUE: BREAKING TASKS INTO MANAGEABLE INTERVALS

Enter the Pomodoro Technique—a method that's both simple and surprisingly effective, especially for those of us who struggle to stay on task. Imagine this: you set a timer for 25 minutes and commit to focusing on a single task: no distractions, no multitasking—just pure, undivided attention. Then, you take a five-minute break to recharge. Rinse and repeat. After four of these cycles, known as Pomodoro's, reward yourself with a longer break. This time management method, developed by Francesco Cirillo in the 1980s, is like the espresso shot of productivity boosts. It's particularly beneficial for ADHD brains, which often crave structure and short bursts of focus.

The Pomodoro Technique is a game-changer because it breaks tasks into manageable chunks, which helps reduce overwhelm. It also helps to improve focus, allowing you to dive deep into tasks without the usual brain fog. The structured work intervals create a sense of urgency that keeps you motivated and accountable. Plus, it prevents burnout by encouraging regular breaks so you don't feel like a wet noodle by the end of the day. The technique is like a lighthouse, guiding you through the stormy seas of procrastination and indecision.

So, how do you get started with the Pomodoro Technique? It's as easy as pie. First, pick a task that needs your attention. Set a timer for 25 minutes, which is one Pomodoro, and dive in with laser-like focus. When the timer rings, take a five-minute break. This could be as simple as stretching, grabbing a snack, or doing a quick lap around your living room. After four Pomodoro's, reward yourself with a longer break of 15 to 30 minutes. This is your time to relax and recharge before diving back into the next task.

To maximize your Pomodoro sessions, choose specific, manageable tasks. Instead of tackling a vague goal like "cleaning the house," break it down into smaller tasks like "wiping the kitchen counters" or "sorting laundry." By focusing on one thing at a time, you're less likely to get distracted by other tasks demanding your attention. Create a distraction-free zone during your Pomodoro intervals. Turn off notifications, close unnecessary tabs, and let your housemates know you're in focus mode. After each session, take a moment to evaluate what you accomplished and adjust your plan if needed. This reflection helps you identify what worked well and what didn't, allowing you to continuously improve your focus and productivity.

The Pomodoro Technique is versatile and can be used for various tasks. It's perfect for reviewing and organizing emails, where you can dedicate time to clearing your inbox. It's also great for writing reports or articles, helping you maintain a steady flow of ideas without getting sidetracked. If your home needs a little TLC, use the technique to clean specific areas, such as a bathroom or a closet. Even study sessions for exams can benefit from this method, as it encourages dedicated focus and regular breaks, keeping your brain sharp and engaged.

Interactive Exercise: Try the Pomodoro Technique

1. Select a Task: Choose a task you've been putting off. It could be anything from organizing your digital files to tackling a work project.
2. Set Your Timer: Use a timer app or a kitchen timer and set it for 25 minutes.
3. Focus: Dive into your task with full attention, ignoring distractions.
4. Take a Break: When the timer rings, take a five-minute break. Stretch, breathe, relax.

5. Repeat: After four rounds of Pomodoro, take a longer break. Reflect on your progress and adjust your strategy if needed.

TIME BLOCKING FOR ADHD: STRUCTURING YOUR DAY FOR SUCCESS

Time blocking is like creating a blueprint for your day. It's a method that allows you to divide your day into chunks and assign each block to a specific activity or task. Imagine your day as a big jigsaw puzzle, and time blocking helps you neatly fit the pieces. For those of us with ADHD, this technique can be a lifesaver. It reduces decision fatigue—the mental exhaustion from constantly deciding what to do next. That nagging question, "What should I focus on now?" With time blocking, you've already decided ahead of time, so you can focus more on doing and less on determining. This structured approach can boost productivity by providing a clear plan, reducing the day's chaos into manageable segments.

To set up a time-blocked schedule, start by identifying your daily tasks. Write them down—everything from feeding the cat to preparing for that big presentation. Once you've got your list, categorize these tasks. Think of them like sorting laundry: whites, colors, delicates—group similar tasks together, like emails, meetings, or creative work. Next, allocate specific time blocks for each type of activity. If you're a morning person, you might dedicate the early hours to deep-focus work, reserving the afternoon for meetings or collaborative tasks. Don't forget to include buffer times. These are your safety nets for unexpected events or transitions between tasks. They're like the extra time you give yourself to get to an appointment, just in case you hit traffic. Trust me, these can be the difference between a smooth day and one where you're constantly playing catch-up.

Flexibility is critical when it comes to time blocking. Life happens, and sometimes your perfectly planned schedule needs a tweak. Be realistic about how long tasks will take. If you think a task will take 30 minutes, maybe give it 45. This extra padding helps prevent stress if things run over, and it allows for breaks and downtime, too. You're not a robot; you need moments to recharge. Adjust your time blocks based on your priorities and energy levels. Some days, you might find your energy plummeting mid-afternoon. That's okay—shift that creative work block to a time when you're more energized, and use the lull for something less demanding.

Let's look at some examples of effective time-blocked schedules. Imagine your morning routine: wake up, exercise, have breakfast, and plan out your day. You might start with a block for physical activity, breakfast, and a quiet moment to set your intentions. Next, your workday schedule could include focused work sessions in the morning when your mind is sharpest. Schedule meetings or collaborative work for the afternoon, interspersed with breaks to stretch and clear your mind. As the day winds down, create an evening routine that includes relaxation, family time, and preparing for tomorrow. Maybe it's a block for cooking dinner, another for unwinding with a book or a show, and finally, a short block for setting up the next day's schedule.

Time blocking can transform your day from a chaotic rush to a well-choreographed dance. It's like having a personal assistant manage your schedule, except that assistant is you—empowered with a plan. The key is to be intentional about allocating your time, ensuring you spend it on what matters most.

PRIORITIZING TASKS: WHAT TO DO FIRST WHEN EVERYTHING FEELS URGENT

So, you've got a mountain of tasks, each shouting louder than the next for your attention. It's like being in a room full of toddlers, each demanding a cookie simultaneously. For those with ADHD, this scenario isn't just a one-off; it's a daily occurrence. The chaos of trying to decide what to tackle first can be paralyzing. Poor prioritization can turn your productivity into a tangled mess, leaving you spinning your wheels yet going nowhere. But fear not. There's hope in the form of task prioritization. It's not just about getting things done; it's about getting the right things done. Imagine having a clear action plan where you know exactly what to focus on and when. That's the beauty of prioritization. It's your GPS through the maze, helping you cut through the clutter and channel your energy where it truly matters.

Now, let's talk about techniques. The Eisenhower Matrix, for example, is a tool that helps you distinguish between urgent and important tasks. Picture a box divided into four squares. Tasks that are both urgent and important go in the top left. These are your fires—handle them first. Important but not urgent tasks fit in the top right. They deserve your attention but won't explode if you hold off for a bit. Urgent but not vital tasks, which can often be delegated, slide into the bottom left. Finally, the bottom right is for functions that are neither urgent nor important—these are the ones you can skip or do later.

Then there's the ABCDE Method, which ranks tasks by importance and urgency. You label each task with a letter from A (most important) to E (least important). You tackle all your A tasks before moving on to B, and so forth. It's a simple yet effective way to keep your priorities straight. And who could forget the Ivy Lee Method? This technique involves choosing the six most crucial tasks for the day, writing them down, and focusing solely on the first task until it's done before moving on to the next. It's about narrowing your focus to what truly matters rather than getting lost in the sea of possibilities.

To put these strategies into action, start by creating a task list. Write down everything you need to do, no matter how small. Once your list is complete, it's time to categorize. Assess each task's urgency and importance. Ask yourself: Will it matter in a week? A month? Then, focus on high-priority tasks first. Delegate or postpone those that fall lower on the list. It's like triaging your workload—ensuring that the most critical tasks get your immediate attention while others wait their turn.

Take the Eisenhower Matrix, for instance. Use it to plan a workday by placing urgent client calls and project deadlines in the urgent-important quadrant. Tasks like long-term planning might sit in the important-but-not-urgent square, while replying to non-urgent emails could fall into the urgent-but-not-important category, perfect for delegation.

Or consider a busy weekend where the ABCDE Method shines. Rank your tasks: perhaps grocery shopping is an A, meal prepping a B, and that impulse to reorganize the garage is a C. Prioritize accordingly, ensuring that what truly needs doing gets done. With the Ivy Lee Method, imagine you have a project deadline looming. List the six essential tasks you must complete and attack them individually, maintaining focus and progress.

By weaving these techniques into your daily routine, you'll find that the cacophony of demands fades, replaced by a symphony of productivity. Tasks become clearer, and the path forward becomes less daunting. Prioritization isn't just a tool; it's a lifeline that helps you navigate the complex world of adult ADHD, ensuring you spend your time wisely and effectively.

BATTLING PROCRASTINATION: TECHNIQUES TO GET STARTED AND STAY FOCUSED

Procrastination and ADHD often go hand in hand, like peanut butter and jelly, but with less deliciousness and more frustration. The link between ADHD and procrastination is rooted in the brain's executive dysfunction, which can make getting started on tasks feel like trying to push a boulder uphill. It's not just about being lazy or indecisive. It's about how your brain processes tasks and the emotions that come with them. Executive dysfunction plays a significant role, making prioritizing what needs to be done difficult. Emotional factors like fear of failure or the relentless pursuit of perfectionism add a layer of complexity. Starting a task and not doing it perfectly can be paralyzing, leading to avoidance and, you guessed it, procrastination.

But fear not, for there are strategies to combat this productivity thief. One effective technique is to break tasks into smaller, manageable steps—a plan that feels like putting training wheels on a bicycle. It makes the ride less intimidating and more achievable. Instead of telling yourself to "clean the kitchen," narrow it down to "clear the dining table" or "wipe the counters." This approach reduces overwhelm and makes each step feel doable. External cues and reminders are also your friends here. Setting alarms, using sticky notes, or having a digital assistant remind you can keep tasks on your radar. These cues act like little nudges that push you into action, helping you maintain focus and momentum.

Rewarding yourself for progress is another powerful tool. Think of it as a way to trick your brain into associating tasks with positive outcomes. It doesn't have to be extravagant—a cup of your favorite coffee or a quick scroll through social media can do the trick. The key is to celebrate completion, no matter how small, to build a positive feedback loop that encourages continued effort.

Now, let's explore the concept of "micro-tasks." These are bite-sized actions that make tasks less daunting and easier to start. Imagine tasks so small that they seem almost too easy to ignore. Writing the first sentence of an email, sorting one file, or cleaning one shelf, are micro-tasks. Focusing on these tiny actions, you create a sense of accomplishment that can propel you forward. It's like laying one brick at a time to build a house. Each micro-task is a step toward completing the bigger picture.

Real-life stories of overcoming procrastination can be incredibly motivating. Take Sarah, a student who struggled with study habits. The mountain of notes and books felt overbearing until she started to break her study sessions into micro-tasks. She'd set a goal to read just one paragraph or summarize one page. This approach transformed her study habits, allowing her to progress without feeling overwhelmed. My friend's husband, Tom, a professional found his productivity spiraling due to procrastination. He implemented a system of rewards, treating himself to a short walk or a favorite podcast episode after completing tasks. This method rekindled his motivation, enabling him to tackle work with renewed focus and enthusiasm.

As you've read through these strategies, remember that battling procrastination isn't about eliminating it. It's about managing it, finding ways to get started, and staying focused despite the distractions. Procrastination may never disappear completely, but with these techniques, you can reduce its grip on your life and boost your productivity meaningfully.

4
ROOM-BY-ROOM DECLUTTERING STRATEGIES

What if; you open the front door, and instead of stepping into a serene sanctuary, you're met with chaos? Shoes, coats, and the mysterious pile of mail that seems to breed overnight. It's like your entryway has a life of its own, determined to trip you up before you've even kicked off your shoes. But fear not, for this chapter is your trusty sidekick in taming the wild beast that is your entryway. This often-overlooked space is more than just a pass-through; it's the gateway to your home and sets the tone for everything beyond it. You want it to say, "Welcome, come on in," rather than, "Beware, chaos ahead!"

A clutter-free entryway does wonders for your daily routine. Imagine breezing in and out without the obstacle course of misplaced footwear and forgotten umbrellas. First impressions matter, and your entryway is the first thing guests see. A welcoming, tidy space says, "I've got it together," even if the rest of the house disagrees. A clear entryway facilitates easy entry and exit for you, your family, and visitors, making mornings less of a mad dash and more of a calm stroll. Who knew a tidy entryway could be the secret to starting your day, right?

So, how do you transform this often chaotic zone into a functional and inviting space? Start by removing unnecessary items. That pile of shoes you haven't worn since the last decade? They can go. Next, sort and categorize what's left. Group similar items together—coats with coats, shoes with shoes, and keys with anything that's not shoes. This is your chance to channel your inner Marie Kondo, keeping only what sparks joy—or at least serves a purpose.

Now, let's talk storage solutions. Wall-mounted hooks are your friends here, perfect for coats and bags that need a home. Consider a shoe rack or a bench with storage underneath. Not only does this provide a place to sit while you lace up, but it also hides the clutter. Baskets or trays are excellent for corralling keys and mail, keeping them off surfaces and within easy reach. If you're feeling fancy, a vintage piece of furniture can add style and function, offering storage while serving as a statement piece. Think of your entryway as the appetizer to your home—it should be both functional and inviting, setting the stage for the main course that is your living space.

Maintaining an organized entryway doesn't have to be a Herculean task. Implement a daily or weekly tidying routine. Spend a few minutes each day putting things back in their designated spots, and you'll prevent clutter from accumulating. Assign specific places for frequently used items. Your keys? They belong in that cute little dish by the door. The dog leash? It's right there on the hook. Giving everything a home eliminates the frantic search that inevitably happens when running late.

Interactive Element: Entryway Makeover Checklist

- Identify: Spend a few minutes observing your entryway. What items are necessary, and what can be removed?
- Sort and Categorize: Group-like items. Keep only what serves a purpose or brings joy.
- Storage Solutions: Decide on storage options that fit your space and style. Consider hooks, racks, and baskets.
- Daily Routine: Set a timer for five minutes daily to tidy up.

Following these steps will turn your entryway from a chaotic catch-all into a harmonious haven. Your future self will thank you every time you step through the door, greeted by a sense of calm and order rather than chaos and confusion. So, roll up those sleeves and get started—the entryway of your dreams awaits!

KITCHEN CHAOS: ORGANIZING FOR EFFICIENCY AND EASE

Ah, the kitchen—where culinary dreams either come to life or crash in a heap of misplaced measuring cups and forgotten ingredients. For many, it's the heart of the home, a bustling hub that sees more foot traffic than a shopping mall during the January sales. But with significant usage comes great clutter. Between the pots, pans, spices, and gadgets, it's no wonder the kitchen often feels like chaos incarnate. This high-traffic area demands constant attention and, without some semblance of order, can transform even the most straightforward meal prep into a quest for the Holy Grail. An organized kitchen, however, can make all the difference. It streamlines meal preparation, turning cooking into the joyful experience it's meant to be. Imagine reaching for a spatula without sending a tower of Tupperware crashing down. Heaven.

To reclaim your kitchen, start with a clean slate. Empty those cabinets and drawers as if you're staging a miniature kitchen apocalypse. Yes, it might look worse before it gets better, but trust the process. Once everything's out, give those shelves and drawers a good scrub. You'll be surprised at what's accumulated there, like finding an archaeological dig site of expired spices and long-lost gadgets. Next, sort and categorize your kitchen items: group similar things together—baking supplies, cooking utensils, cutlery. As you sort, be ruthless when discarding expired or unused items. If it's been sitting there since the last time bell-bottoms were in style, it's probably time to say goodbye.

With the clutter cleared, it's time to think about storage. Drawer dividers are a magician's trick for utensils, keeping them from turning into a tangled mess. Clear containers are your new best friends for your pantry. Not only do they keep things tidy, but they also let you know when you're running low on essentials. Lazy Susan's can bring a touch of elegance to spice storage, spinning your way to the perfect pinch of paprika. And please keep vertical storage solutions for pots and pans in mind. Hanging them up or using a pegboard can free up precious shelf space in your cabinets.

Keeping your kitchen organized is an ongoing endeavor. Regularly review and purge pantry items. Implement a meal planning system to streamline your shopping and cooking processes. Knowing what's on the docket for dinner can prevent those last-minute, stress-filled rummages through the fridge. And remember, clear countertops are happy countertops. Keep them free from clutter by designating specific places for frequently used items. That way, you can glide through your kitchen like a culinary wizard, easily whipping up meals.

Of course, maintaining this newfound order takes a bit of effort. Develop a habit of tidying up after each meal. Wipe down surfaces, return items to their designated spots, and give yourself a high-five for a job well done. It's all about creating routines that make organization second nature. You might even enjoy the process, relishing the satisfaction of a kitchen ready to rise to any culinary challenge. So, roll up your sleeves, put on your favorite playlist, and transform your kitchen chaos into a harmonious haven where creativity can thrive.

THE LIVING ROOM: TURNING A HIGH-TRAFFIC AREA INTO A CALM RETREAT

The living room is where life happens—movie nights, coffee chats, and lazy Sunday afternoons. It's the heart of social interactions and relaxation, yet often it resembles more of a storage room than a sanctuary. A clutter-free living room enhances both relaxation and social interactions, creating a space where family and guests feel welcomed and at ease. Reducing visual clutter is like lifting a weight off your shoulders; it turns your living room into a haven where you can unwind without the nagging reminder of things left undone. Imagine: sitting on your couch with a good book, surrounded by neatly arranged decor and not a random sock in sight. Bliss, right?

To achieve this serene setting, you need a game plan for decluttering. Start by removing unnecessary items and furniture. That oversized chair you never sit in? It might be time to say goodbye once you've cleared some space, sort and categorize what's left. Group similar items—books, electronics, for example. This helps visualize what you have and what might be in excess. Now comes the fun part: deciding on a layout that maximizes space and functionality. Consider the flow of movement through the room. You want to create pathways that are easy to navigate, allowing for free movement without dodging obstacles.

Storage solutions are efficient here. Shelving units are fantastic for books and decor, offering storage and a chance to showcase your personality. Storage ottomans or coffee tables with hidden compartments are perfect for stashing away TV remotes and magazines with a habit of multiplying. A media center is not just for aesthetics; it can corral electronics and cables, keeping them organized and out of sight. Imagine a living room where everything has its place, where you don't have to dig through a pile of magazines to find the TV remote. It's not just a dream—it's entirely achievable.

Maintaining this newfound order requires some commitment but pays off in spades. Implement daily or weekly tidying routines. Spend a few minutes each day putting things back where they belong. Designate specific spots for frequently used items. The remote has a home, the magazines have a basket, and that cozy throw blanket isn't just tossed haphazardly on the couch. Rotating decor and seasonal items can also keep the space fresh and vibrant. Swapping out a few pieces of art or changing up the couch pillows can breathe new life into the room without needing a full redesign.

You might be wondering how to make this happen without feeling overwhelmed. The key is to start small and build momentum. Tackle one corner of the room at a time, or dedicate just 15 minutes a day to tidying up. As you see progress, that motivation will grow, and soon you'll have a living room that's not only organized but also a joy to be in. Once again, the goal isn't perfection; it's about creating a space that supports your lifestyle. A living room that invites you to sit, relax, and enjoy the company of loved ones without the constant buzz of clutter in the background.

BEDROOM BLISS: CREATING A RESTFUL SANCTUARY

You know that feeling when you collapse into bed after a long day, hoping to drift off into peaceful slumber, only to find yourself staring at the ceiling, overwhelmed by the surrounding mess? It's like trying to meditate in the middle of a circus. An organized bedroom is more than just nice sheets and plumped pillows; it's your retreat, a place to recharge and escape the chaos of the outside world. A clutter-free bedroom can significantly enhance sleep quality and overall well-being, transforming it into a restful place rather than a reminder of unfinished chores. Imagine walking into your room and immediately feeling a sense of calm wash over you. That's the power of a tidy, organized space, where visual clutter is minimized, and serenity reigns supreme.

To achieve this sanctuary, try removing unnecessary items and furniture. That chair that's become a makeshift wardrobe? It's time for it to find a new purpose. By decluttering, you're creating a space that invites relaxation rather than distraction. Next, sort and categorize your clothing and personal items. It's like a treasure hunt, but instead of gold doubloons, you're rediscovering that long-lost sweater you love. Arrange similar items together. This helps with organization and makes it easier to find what you need. Deciding on a layout that maximizes space and functionality is crucial. You want to create a flow that feels natural and uncluttered, allowing for easy movement and access to everyday essentials.

Now, let's talk about storage solutions for maintaining that sense of order. Under-bed storage containers are a fantastic way to utilize often-overlooked space. They're perfect for storing off-season clothes or extra linens, keeping them out of sight but easily accessible. Closet organizers and shelving units can turn a chaotic closet into a beacon of order, providing designated spots for everything from shoes to hats. Bedside tables with drawers or shelves offer space for nighttime necessities, ensuring your book or glass of water is always within arm's reach. Decorative baskets are functional and add a touch of style, perfect for stashing miscellaneous items like charging cables or extra blankets.

Just as with the other rooms in your house, keeping your bedroom organized is an ongoing process, but it doesn't have to be a chore. Implement daily or weekly tidying routines to prevent clutter from creeping back in. Spend a few minutes each day putting things back in their designated spots, and you'll save yourself from a weekend of cleaning marathons. Establish a laundry system for clean and dirty clothes so they don't end up scattered across the floor like a modern art exhibition. Use a hamper for dirty clothes and a designated space for clean ones awaiting folding. By keeping surfaces clear and clutter-free, you maintain the tranquility of your sanctuary, allowing your bedroom to be the peaceful retreat it was always meant to be.

As you lie back on your freshly made bed, with everything in its place, you'll feel the stress from the day melt away. A well-organized bedroom isn't just about aesthetics; it's about creating a space that supports relaxation. When your surroundings are calm, your mind can follow suit, leading to better sleep and improved mood. Use your new mindset and skills to transform your bedroom into a serene sanctuary, setting the stage for restful nights and refreshed mornings.

5
ORGANIZING PERSONAL SPACES

Ah, the closet—a space that should be a sanctuary of style and simplicity but often turns into a Bermuda Triangle for clothes you vaguely remember buying. You know the drill: you open those doors, and it's like a fashion avalanche, with shirts, pants, and the occasional shoe threatening to bury you alive. But fear not, my fellow ADHDer, organizing your closet can transform your morning routine from a frantic fashion show into a serene sartorial selection. Imagine opening your closet and immediately spotting that perfect shirt without wading through a sea of fabric. It's like having a personal boutique at home, where everything fits, and matches and nothing is hiding behind that questionable 80s windbreaker you swore you'd wear again.

An organized closet doesn't just save you time; it reduces stress and makes you feel in charge of your personal space. No more Monday morning meltdowns trying to find that one pair of matching socks. With a well-organized closet, outfit selection becomes a breeze, freeing up your mornings for more important decisions—like whether you should have toast or cereal. Also, knowing exactly where everything is means less time searching for items, leaving you more time to hit the snooze button. An organized wardrobe gives you a sense of order and calm, creating a serene environment that can enhance focus and productivity.

Now, let's dig into the nitty-gritty of closet decluttering. Start by emptying your closet. Yes, it will look like a tornado hit your bedroom, but trust me, it's the best way. Once everything is out, give that closet a good clean. Dust the shelves and vacuum the floor. You might even find a long-lost sock or two. Next, sort your clothing into three piles: keep, donate, and discard. Keep items you wear regularly or that spark joy. Donate pieces that are in good condition but haven't seen daylight in over a year. And discard anything that's seen better days—stains, holes, or that shirt that shrunk in the wash (or maybe you grew a bit).

Once you've sorted, it's time to evaluate each item based on its frequency of use, fit, and condition. If you haven't worn it in a year, it might be time to let it go. Seasonal rotation is key to maximizing space. Store winter clothes during summer and vice versa. This frees up the room and keeps your wardrobe fresh and current. Use garment bags to protect delicate or formal wear, and consider storage solutions like Zip Top Storage Boxes or Cube Storage Bins for organization.

On to organizing solutions. Invest in quality hangers, bins, and shelf dividers to tidy your closet. Implement a color-coded system for hanging clothes—it's not just for aesthetics but also to help you easily find what you're looking for.

Installing additional shelves or rods can provide extra storage space, making room for those new pieces you can't resist. Clear storage boxes for shoes and accessories are a lifesaver, allowing you to see precisely what you have without pulling them out and opening them up.

Keeping your closet organized is a marathon, not a sprint. Regularly review and purge items to prevent clutter from creeping back in. A one-in-one-out policy for new clothing purchases is a good method to keep quantity under control. Bought a new dress? Say goodbye to an old one. This keeps your closet from overflowing and ensures you only hold on to pieces you love. Maintaining a laundry schedule helps prevent that dreaded pile-up of clean clothes waiting to be folded and put away. With these strategies, you're well on your way to a closet that's organized and a joy to use.

Reflection Section: Your Closet Goals

- Visualize Your Ideal Closet: Imagine your organized closet. What's hanging where? What colors do you see?
- Set a Decluttering Date: Choose a day to tackle your closet and commit to it.
- Plan for Maintenance: What will it take to keep your closet organized? Weekly reviews? A monthly purge? Write it down.

BATHROOM BASICS: STREAMLINING YOUR MORNING ROUTINE

Do you wake up in the morning and go to the bathroom, only to be greeted by a cluttered countertop of half-empty shampoo bottles, a tangled mess of hair ties, and toothpaste tubes that have somehow multiplied overnight? It's the kind of chaos that can turn your morning routine into a frantic scavenger hunt. An organized bathroom, however, is a game-changer. It's like stepping into a spa every morning, where everything has its place, and you can find the hairbrush without tearing the room apart. A streamlined bathroom reduces the time spent searching for toiletries and sets a calming tone for your day, ensuring you start with a sense of peace rather than panic. Plus, an organized bathroom makes cleaning and maintenance a breeze, sparing you from those dreaded deep-cleaning marathons when things get out of hand.

So, how do you transform your bathroom from cluttered chaos into a serene sanctuary? Start by emptying all cabinets, drawers, and shelves. Yes, everything needs to come out. It might feel like you've unleashed a small hurricane, but trust me, it's necessary. Once your bathroom looks like a cyclone hit it, sort items into three categories: keep, discard, and relocate. Keep the essentials you use daily, discard expired or broken items, and relocate anything that doesn't belong in the bathroom. Cleaning all surfaces and storage areas is crucial. Wipe down the shelves, scrub the sink, and ensure your bathroom sparkles like a diamond. You'll be surprised at how refreshing a clean slate can be.

Next, let's talk about storage solutions. Drawer dividers are perfect for organizing makeup and toiletries. They prevent that dreaded moment when you're rummaging through a sea of lipsticks to find your favorite shade. Over-the-door organizers offer additional storage without taking up precious floor space. Use clear containers for cotton swabs, pads, and other small items. Not only do they keep things tidy, but they also allow you to see precisely what you have left, preventing those last-minute runs to the store. Shower caddies and shelves are perfect for keeping bathroom essentials within reach. No more slipping in the shower while grabbing the shampoo from the far corner. These solutions turn your bathroom into a model of efficiency and elegance, where everything has its place and is easily accessible.

Maintaining an organized bathroom is an ongoing task, but it doesn't have to feel like punishment. Regularly review and purge expired or unused items. It's astonishing how quickly things pile up when you're not looking. Implement a daily wipe-down routine for surfaces. A quick wipe here, a rinse there, and you'll prevent grime from building up. Keep frequently used items within easy reach. The less time you spend digging through drawers, the more time you have to enjoy your morning coffee.

Interactive Element: Bathroom Organization Checklist

- Empty Everything: Clear out all cabinets, drawers, and shelves. Yes, even the ones you've been avoiding.
- Sort and Categorize: Decide what to keep, discard, and relocate. Be ruthless with expired products.

- Clean All Surfaces: Wipe down shelves, scrub the sink, and tackle any stubborn spots.
- Implement Storage Solutions: Use drawer dividers, over-the-door organizers, and clear containers to keep everything tidy.
- Maintain Regularly: Schedule a quick daily wipe-down, and purge items monthly to prevent clutter from returning.

By following these steps, you'll transform your bathroom into a space that doesn't just function—it flourishes. Your mornings will be smoother, your days brighter, and your bathroom'll look like the kind of place you'd actually want to spend time in.

HOME OFFICE HARMONY: CREATING A PRODUCTIVE WORKSPACE

You are sitting at your desk, ready to tackle the day. You look around at your workspace only to see a mountain of papers, stray pens, and those mysterious cables that seem to entangle when you turn your back. Your home office has declared mutiny, determined to derail your productivity before you even start. But fear not, a well-organized home office can be yours. An orderly workspace isn't just about looking pretty; it's about enhancing productivity and focus. When your desk is clear, your mind follows suit, reducing distractions and increasing efficiency. It's like a mental feng shui that creates a professional environment where work tasks become more manageable. Simplifying document management and task tracking means less time hunting for that contract you swear you just saw and more time getting things done.

So, how do you transform your home office from mayhem to masterful? Start by creating three 'holding' areas, keep, discard, and file. Put everything from your desk, shelves, and workspace into one of the appropriate areas. If it's outdated, irrelevant, or you didn't remember you had it, let it go! Remember, like the other rooms, be ruthless with your decisions. Once everything is out, clean all the surfaces and equipment. Dust off those shelves, wipe down your desk and ensure your computer screen is free from smudges. A clean slate is a blank canvas for productivity.

Now, let's talk about organizing solutions. Filing cabinets and folders are ideal when it comes to document management. They keep essential papers neatly categorized and easily accessible. Desk organizers are perfect for pens, paper, and other small items that tend to scatter like confetti. Cable management solutions are lifesavers for reducing wire clutter. Velcro ties, clips, or even a simple cable box can prevent the dreaded spaghetti junction of tangled cords. Shelving units are excellent for books and reference materials, providing a home for everything that doesn't belong on your desk. Imagine a workspace where everything has its place, and you're not constantly searching for that elusive file.

Maintaining an organized home office is a continuous process and requires the exact skillset you have already applied in other areas and it doesn't have to be overwhelming. Implement a daily or weekly filing routine. Spend a few minutes each day or week sorting through papers and putting them in their designated spots. Keeping the desk surface clear of unnecessary items is key. It's tempting to leave things "just for now," but that's how clutter creeps back in. Regularly reviewing and purging outdated documents prevents your files from turning into a paper graveyard.

Your home office should be where you feel inspired and ready to take on any challenge. With these strategies, you can create a productive workspace that supports your goals and keeps distractions at bay. So, roll up your sleeves, grab a cup of coffee, and get ready to transform your home office into a place of productivity and focus.

CRAFT AND HOBBY AREAS: ORGANIZING YOUR CREATIVE OUTLETS

Imagine you're ready to dive into your latest craft project, excited and inspired. But as you step into your craft room or hobby area, your enthusiasm quickly deflates. The chaos of tangled yarn, scattered beads, and paintbrushes buried under stacks of paper is enough to squash any creative spark. A well-organized craft area can be as energizing as a double shot of espresso. It transforms your workspace into an oasis where creativity flows effortlessly and enjoyment takes center stage. With everything in its place, you'll spend less time hunting for that elusive pair of scissors and more time bringing your ideas to life. Plus, making the most of your available space means you can spread out and let your creativity run wild without constantly bumping into clutter.

Now, let's roll up our sleeves and tackle the mess head-on. By emptying all storage areas, from shelves to drawers, and spreading everything out, it might look like a colorful explosion, but this is where the magic happens. Once you've laid everything bare, it's time to sort through the materials. Create three piles: keep, donate, and discard. Be honest with yourself—if you haven't touched those supplies since your last creative binge, consider letting them go. Cleaning surfaces and storage containers is crucial. Dust off shelves, wipe down surfaces and make sure your space is as fresh as your next idea. You'll be surprised how a clean slate revitalizes your creative spirit.

When it comes to organizing solutions, think of practicality and accessibility. Clear bins and boxes are ideal for different types of materials. They let you see exactly what you have, so you're not buying duplicates of things you already own. Pegboards or wall-mounted organizers are excellent for tools and supplies, keeping everything visible and within reach. Imagine reaching for a paintbrush without dislodging an avalanche of markers. Labeling systems are your best friend here. They make identifying materials a breeze, saving you time and frustration. Rolling carts or portable storage solutions offer flexibility, allowing you to move supplies to wherever inspiration strikes. It's like having a mobile studio that adapts to your needs.

To maintain an organized craft area, regularly review and purge unused items. Set aside time every few months to reassess your supplies and clear out anything gathering dust. Implement a cleanup routine after each project. Spend a few minutes returning materials to their designated spots so your next creative session starts with a clean space. Keep frequently used materials within easy reach. The less time you spend rifling through boxes, the more time you have to immerse yourself in your creative pursuits.

An organized craft area is more than just a tidy space; it's a launchpad for creativity. When your environment supports your creative process, you'll be more inspired and eager to create. So, transform your cluttered chaos into an organized oasis and watch your creativity soar to new heights. As we move forward, in the next chapter, we'll explore the digital realm, tackling the clutter on our screens and devices. Your journey to an organized life continues, one space at a time.

6

DIGITAL DECLUTTERING

If you open your email, instead of a neat, manageable list, you're greeted by a wall of unread messages, each one clamoring for your attention like a toddler in a candy store. It makes anyone want to throw their laptop out the window. But fear not because today we're tackling the digital chaos of email with a concept called Inbox Zero. Now, before you roll your eyes, thinking it's just another unrealistic goal, let's break it down. Inbox Zero isn't about obsessively maintaining an empty inbox at all times. Instead, it's about managing your emails efficiently, reducing stress, and transforming your inbox from a source of anxiety to a productivity powerhouse.

The term Inbox Zero was coined by productivity guru Merlin Mann, who introduced it as a way to minimize our time on emails, allowing us to focus on what matters. With the average person sending and receiving a staggering 121 business emails daily, it's no wonder our inboxes can feel like a black hole. Achieving Inbox Zero means responding to, deleting, or archiving emails immediately, keeping your inbox organized and stress-free. The benefits are clear: reduced time spent on emails, improved focus, and a decreased chance of missing important messages. It's about creating a mindset shift, turning your email from a dreaded chore into a tool that works for you.

So, how do you conquer the email beast and reach Inbox Zero? Start by sorting your emails into categories. Think of it like Marie Kondo-ing your inbox. Create folders for emails requiring action, those for reference, and ones ready to be archived. This way, you can easily find your needs without wading through a sea of messages. Next, be ruthless in deleting unnecessary emails. If it doesn't serve a purpose, let it go. Unsubscribe from spam and newsletters that no longer interest you—they're like digital junk mail, taking up space and attention. Set up filters and rules for incoming emails, directing them to the appropriate folders. This step automates your inbox management, manually reducing the mental load of sorting through each new email.

Establish a routine of daily or weekly email review sessions to maintain Inbox Zero. Think of it as a quick health check for your inbox. During these sessions, apply the two-minute rule: if you can deal with an email in two minutes or less, do it immediately. This prevents tasks from piling up and keeps your inbox manageable. Develop a habit of sorting emails as soon as they arrive. It's like putting dishes away immediately after washing them—much less daunting than letting them stack up.

Email management tools can be game-changers in this endeavor. Consider email clients with advanced sorting features, like Gmail or Microsoft Outlook, which offer labels and filters to streamline your inbox. Tools like Sane Box automatically sort emails into folders, ensuring only the most important ones grab your attention. If you juggle multiple email accounts, apps that consolidate them, like Mailbird or Spark, allow you to manage everything in one place. They're like the Swiss Army knives of email management, equipped with all the features you need to stay organized.

Interactive Exercise: Kickstart Your Inbox Zero

1. Create Folders: Set up folders for action required, reference, and archive in your email client.
2. Automate Sorting: Use filters to direct incoming emails to the correct folders automatically.
3. Unsubscribe: Spend ten minutes unsubscribing from newsletters and spam.
4. Daily Check: Schedule a brief email review session daily. Use the two-minute rule to tackle quick responses.

Armed with these strategies and tools, Inbox Zero becomes achievable, transforming your email from a stressor into an ally in your quest for organized living.

SIMPLIFYING DIGITAL FILES: ORGANIZING YOUR COMPUTER AND CLOUD STORAGE

You know that feeling when your computer desktop resembles a digital junkyard, with random files scattered like confetti after a party? It's like opening your closet and having everything tumble out at once. You might think, "I'll take care of it later," but we both know how that story ends. A well-organized digital filing system is more than just a tidy screen—it's a productivity booster and a stress reducer. Imagine having quick access to essential documents without the digital hide-and-seek. No more wasting precious time searching for files buried in the depths of your hard drive. It's about creating a seamless workflow that allows you to focus on what truly matters, not the chaos lurking in your digital corners.

Start by creating a hierarchical folder structure. Think of it like setting up a filing cabinet where each drawer has a purpose. Top-level folders could be broad categories like "Work," "Personal," or "Finances." Within these, create subfolders for specific projects or themes. For instance, under "Work," you might have folders for "Reports," "Meetings," and "Projects." This structure acts like a roadmap, guiding you directly to what you need without detours. Next, consider your naming conventions. Consistent, descriptive names make it easy to identify files at a glance. Avoid cryptic labels like "Doc1" or "FinalFinalVersion2"—we've all been there. Instead, choose clear names with dates or keywords, like "Annual_Report_2023" or "Vacation_Photos_March."

Sorting files by type, date, or project can also help. Use your computer's file sorting capabilities to group similar files, making them easier to find. Regularly purge outdated or duplicate files to keep your system lean and efficient. It's like cleaning out your closet—if you haven't touched it in a year, it's probably time to let it go. This frees up space and ensures your digital filing system remains relevant and useful.

Maintaining this newfound order requires a bit of diligence. Regularly review and reorganize your files, perhaps as part of a monthly routine. It's like taking your digital system for a tune-up, ensuring everything runs smoothly. Implement a backup routine to prevent data loss. Use cloud services or external drives to create copies of important files. It's your digital insurance policy, providing peace of mind if your computer takes an unexpected sabbatical. Utilizing tags and metadata can also elevate your organization game. These tools allow advanced file sorting, connecting files across folders based on themes or projects. It's like adding a GPS to your digital roadmap, making navigation a breeze.

Digital file management tools are your allies in this organizational quest. Consider file organization software that streamlines the process. Cloud storage solutions like Google Drive or Dropbox offer collaborative features, making file sharing a cinch. They're like the virtual filing cabinets you can access from anywhere, perfect for remote work or group projects. Tools for automatic file backup and synchronization ensure that your files are always up-to-date and accessible, regardless of where you are. Imagine the freedom of knowing that your important documents are just a click away, no matter what device you're using.

With these strategies and tools in place, you're well-equipped to tackle the digital clutter lurking in your life. It's not just about tidying up—it's about reclaiming your time, focus, and peace of mind. So roll up those sleeves and transform your digital space into a beacon of organization and efficiency.

SOCIAL MEDIA DETOX: REDUCING DIGITAL DISTRACTIONS

You know the drill: you sit down with your morning coffee, intending to check a few updates on social media. Suddenly, an hour passes, and you've fallen down a rabbit hole of cat videos and travel blogs. It's almost like time traveling but without the fun of a TARDIS. Social media, for all its connectivity and entertainment, can be a major culprit in digital clutter. The constant pings and notifications can pull your attention in many directions, leaving you feeling scattered and unproductive. It's not just about the time spent scrolling; it's about how these platforms impact your focus and productivity. Studies have shown that excessive social media use can shorten attention spans, making it difficult to concentrate on tasks that require sustained focus. It's like trying to read a novel while someone reads out loud from a different book beside you. Your brain constantly switches gears, leading to fatigue and reduced efficiency.

To reclaim your focus, consider a social media detox. Start by identifying how much time you spend on these platforms. You might be surprised at the hours that slip away. Most smartphones have built-in tools that track screen time, allowing you to see the cold facts of your scrolling habits. Once you've identified your usage, set specific times for social media check-ins. Instead of grazing throughout the day, allocate dedicated slots for catching up on your feeds. This limits distractions and turns social media into a scheduled activity rather than a constant background noise.

Turning off non-essential notifications is another decisive step. Those little red dots and buzzes are designed to grab your attention like a toddler tugging at your sleeve. By silencing these alerts, you create a quieter digital environment that allows you to focus on what truly matters. Use apps like Offtime or AppDetox to further track and limit your social media usage. These tools can help set boundaries, ensuring you don't fall into the trap of endless scrolling.

Maintaining a balanced presence on social media is key to staying connected without feeling overwhelmed. Curate your feed to focus on positive and relevant content. Unfollow accounts that don't add value or bring joy to your life. Think of it as digital decluttering—keeping only what sparks joy. Engage in meaningful interactions rather than passive scrolling. Comment, share, and connect with posts that resonate with you, making your online experience more enriching and intentional. Set boundaries by designating specific times when you're offline, especially during work hours or personal time. This creates a healthier relationship with social media, ensuring it serves you rather than vice versa.

Plenty of tools help manage your social media use more effectively. Apps like StayFree and Social Fever can limit screen time and track usage, providing insights into your habits. If you're managing multiple accounts, tools like Buffer or Hootsuite allow you to schedule and automate posts, keeping your presence active without constant monitoring. Many social media platforms now offer features to manage notifications and content preferences, giving you control of what you see and when.

By taking these steps, you can transform your social media experience from a timesink into a tool that enhances your life. It's about being intentional with your digital interactions and ensuring they align with your goals and values.

MANAGING DIGITAL TASKS: USING APPS AND TOOLS EFFECTIVELY

Ever felt like you're juggling a bunch of flaming torches while riding a unicycle? That's what managing tasks can feel like, especially with ADHD. This is where digital task management apps swoop in like superheroes, ready to save the day. These tools centralize tasks and to-do lists into one neat package, making it easier to keep track of everything from grocery lists to work deadlines. They offer reminders and deadlines, ensuring you don't miss that crucial meeting or forget your friend's birthday. Plus, they facilitate collaboration and project management, making group projects less of a headache and more of a breeze. Imagine having a personal assistant who organizes all your tasks, reminds you when things are due, and even helps you work with others—all without the hefty salary. That's the beauty of digital task management apps.

Choosing the right task management app is like finding the perfect pair of shoes: it must fit your style and purpose. Whether you prefer visual boards like Trello, comprehensive platforms like Asana, or simple task lists like Todoist, there's an app for you. Trello is perfect for visual thinkers who love seeing tasks laid out in a board format. It's like having a digital corkboard for your projects. Asana is great for those who need robust project management tools and team collaboration features. It's like a digital command center where everyone knows their roles. Todoist is fantastic for minimalist users who want a straightforward task list with just enough features to keep them organized. Once you've chosen your app, start by setting up your projects and tasks. Break big goals into manageable tasks, and you'll find that what once felt overwhelming becomes achievable.

Use labels, tags, and priorities to organize tasks. This is like adding color-coded tabs to a binder, making it easy to identify what's urgent, what's next, and what can wait. Integrate your task management app with other productivity tools like calendars and emails. This ensures everything is in sync and prevents the dreaded double-booking or missed deadlines. It's like having a digital brain that keeps everything running smoothly without the risk of forgetting an important detail.

Staying consistent with digital task management is key to reaping its benefits. Regularly review and update your tasks and projects. Think of it as a weekly grooming session for your digital workspace. Set daily or weekly planning sessions to organize tasks, ensuring you're always on top of your game. Use notifications and reminders to stay on track. These little nudges can be lifesavers, ensuring you don't drop any balls.

Popular task management tools are plentiful and versatile. With its visual boards, Trello is perfect for those who thrive on seeing tasks and projects laid out visually. Asana offers powerful collaboration features, making it ideal for team projects and complex tasks. Todoist provides simple and intuitive lists, perfect for keeping track of daily tasks without feeling overwhelmed. Evernote is another great tool, combining note-taking and task management into one cohesive platform. It's like having a digital notebook where you can jot down ideas and track tasks all in one place.

With these tools and strategies, managing digital tasks becomes less about juggling and more about orchestrating a well-planned symphony. You'll find yourself with more time, less stress, and a clearer picture of what needs to be done. As we wrap up this chapter on digital decluttering, remember that the tools and techniques we've discussed are just the beginning. They're stepping stones to creating a more organized, intentional life. Next, we'll explore how to maintain these systems over time, ensuring your newfound order doesn't collapse.

Are you curious about "Organized Living with ADHD Made Simple" but unsure where to start? I'm here to make living with ADHD easy and fun for everyone, and I need your help to reach more people!

Many individuals choose books based on reviews, and that's where you come in. Please support a fellow person in the ADHD community by leaving a review.

It costs you nothing and takes less than a minute, but your words could change someone's journey toward better organization and clarity. Your review could help:

- One more small business provide vital resources for their community.
- One more entrepreneur support their family as they navigate challenges.
- One more employee find meaningful work that resonates with their passions.
- One more client transform their life through effective strategies.
- One more dream come true by empowering individuals with ADHD.

To make a positive impact, simply scan the QR code and leave your review:

https://www.amazon.com/review/create-review?asin=B0DP66FYQH

If you love helping others, you're my kind of person. Thank you from the bottom of my heart for your support!

Warm regards,
Nikki Ramirez

7

Maintenance and Habits

Imagine waking up and starting your day with calm, not chaos. Your space is tidy, your mind is clear, and you're not tripping over yesterday's laundry as you go to the kitchen. Now, if your mornings feel more like a scene from a slapstick comedy, where you're dodging piles of clutter and searching for your keys like a treasure hunter, you're not alone. Creating a sanctuary of order might seem like a distant dream, especially when living with ADHD. But here's the good news: establishing daily routines can be your secret weapon. They transform your home from a cluttered battleground into a peaceful retreat.

Daily routines are like the unsung heroes of an organization. They work quietly in the background, preventing clutter from accumulating and making larger cleaning sessions less daunting. Think of them as the gentle, guiding hand that keeps your space ticking without the need for epic weekend cleaning marathons. Establishing consistent daily habits creates a sense of order and calm in your life. You're not just tidying up your living space; you're decluttering your mind too. This is crucial for adults with ADHD, where routine acts as a scaffold, helping to manage symptoms, improve productivity, and enhance overall well-being (Source 1).

Let's look at some effective daily routines that can seamlessly integrate into your life. Imagine starting your morning by making the bed. It's a small act, but it sets a tone of discipline and completion for the day. Next, spend a few minutes tidying up surfaces. This simple task prevents items from piling up and keeps your space fresh. As the day winds down, focus on clearing the kitchen counters. It's a satisfying ritual that prepares you for a new day, ensuring you wake up to a clean slate. Before heading to bed, organize your work desk and put items back in their designated places. This end-of-day routine brings closure to your workday, allowing you to relax without the nagging thought of unfinished tasks.

The concept of "reset zones" can effect significant changes. You can maintain overall organization with minimal effort by identifying high-traffic areas that need regular attention. Think of your reset zone as a mini oasis that, when maintained, keeps the rest of your home in harmony. Set a timer for 10 to 15 minutes daily to tidy these zones. It's a short, focused activity that pays dividends in maintaining a clutter-free space. Whether it's the entryway, kitchen table, or infamous junk drawer, giving these areas regular attention prevents them from becoming overwhelming.

Staying consistent with daily routines can be challenging, especially when life gets hectic. But fear not because there are strategies to help you stay on track. Use reminders and checklists as your trusty sidekicks. They ensure you don't forget the small tasks that keep your space orderly. Involve family members or housemates in the routines. It's like having a team of superheroes, each with their special powers, working together to keep your home in tip-top shape. And don't forget to reward yourself for sticking to your habits. Acknowledging your efforts reinforces positive behavior, whether it's a cup of your favorite tea or a few minutes of downtime.

Interactive Exercise: Create Your Routine

- Morning Routine: List three small tasks you can do every morning to start your day right. Consider making the bed, tidying surfaces, and a quick kitchen sweep.
- Evening Routine: Identify two tasks to wrap up your day, like clearing counters and organizing your work desk.
- Reset Zones: Choose one high-traffic area to focus on for 10 minutes daily. Write it down and set a timer.
- Rewards: Decide on a small reward for completing your routines. Perhaps a favorite snack or a few minutes of relaxation.

By incorporating these routines, maintaining a clutter-free space will become second nature. Your home will become a sanctuary, allowing you to focus on what truly matters.

WEEKLY AND MONTHLY MAINTENANCE: AVOIDING RE-ACCUMULATION

Ever notice how clutter seems to have a life of its own, like that friend who overstays their welcome? You tidy up, blink twice, and suddenly, there's a stack of papers where a clean desk used to be. This is where regular maintenance comes into play. Think of weekly and monthly tasks as your weapon against clutter creep. They help you catch and address issues before they snowball into overwhelming heaps that take over your space and sanity. Regular maintenance ensures that the systems you've painstakingly put in place continue to hum along smoothly, like a well-oiled machine.

A weekly maintenance routine is like giving your home a mini spa day. It's about keeping things fresh and under control without spending your entire weekend cleaning. Start with reviewing and organizing mail and paperwork. Instead of letting letters pile up on the counter, tackle them once a week. Sort through them, pay bills, file important documents, and shred what you don't need. Next, turn your attention to the refrigerator and pantry. Check expiration dates, wipe down shelves, and organize items so you know exactly what's in stock. This keeps your kitchen clean and prevents those awkward moments of discovering a yogurt that expired three months ago. Dusting and vacuuming high-traffic areas is another key task. Think of it as keeping the home's arteries clear, ensuring that dust bunnies don't morph into dust monsters. Finally, take a moment to rotate seasonal items and clothing. This keeps your wardrobe and storage spaces relevant and uncluttered, making it easier to find what you need when you need it.

Monthly maintenance is like a deep-cleaning reboot for your home. It's about tackling those tasks that don't need weekly attention but still require some love. Start with a deep clean of specific areas like bathrooms and kitchen appliances. Scrub those tiles, descale the kettle, and clean the oven well. It's not glamorous, but it makes a world of difference. Next, review and purge digital files and emails. Technology clutter is real; it can bog down your devices just as much as physical clutter bogs down your home. Delete unnecessary files, organize photos, and empty your inbox. Lastly, check and restock household supplies. List essentials like cleaning products, toiletries, and pantry staples. This ensures you're never caught off guard without toilet paper at the worst possible moment.

Creating a maintenance schedule is a bit like setting up a personal assistant to remind you of what needs doing and when. Using a calendar or planner to schedule maintenance tasks, whether it's a wall calendar or a digital app, having a visual reminder helps keep you accountable. Set reminders for monthly deep-cleaning sessions. A little nudge from your phone can go a long way in ensuring you don't forget. Breaking down larger tasks into manageable segments is crucial. Instead of dedicating an entire day to cleaning, instead split it into smaller chunks. Maybe you tackle the bathroom one day and the kitchen the next. This approach makes tasks less daunting and more achievable, leaving you more time to do the things you love.

HABIT STACKING: BUILDING NEW HABITS INTO EXISTING ROUTINES

You've probably heard the old saying about how it's tough to teach an old dog new tricks. Well, whoever came up with that hadn't met the genius of habit stacking. This nifty little concept is about attaching new habits to existing ones, making them easier to adopt and maintain. Think of it as Velcroing a new habit onto a well-established routine. The beauty of habit stacking lies in its simplicity. By leveraging the behaviors you already have, you create a seamless transition for new habits to stick. It's like sneaking vegetables into a kid's favorite dish—they're more likely to eat it without realizing it. This method works wonders for those who struggle with consistency because it builds on the familiar, using the existing neural pathways in your brain to support new actions. Habit stacking is a brilliant strategy, especially for those with ADHD, where the challenge often lies in starting and maintaining new behaviors.

So, how do you put habit stacking into practice, especially when it comes to keeping your space organized? Let's start with the morning coffee routine. While waiting for that lifesaving elixir to brew, sneak in a five-minute declutter session. It's incredible what you can accomplish in those few minutes—tossing out expired coupons, organizing mail, or simply wiping down the counter. Another example is incorporating a quick desk tidy-up at the end of your workday. Before you shut down your computer, spend a few minutes clearing papers and putting pens back in their holders. It's a small act that leaves your workspace fresh for the next day. And let's not forget folding laundry. Pair this often-dreaded task with watching your favorite TV show. Before you know it, you've got neat piles of clothes and a few episodes under your belt. These small adjustments make the organization feel less like a chore and more like an integrated part of your day.

Creating a habit stack is like assembling a personalized toolkit that sets you up for success. Start by identifying existing routines and behaviors. What do you do every day without fail? Maybe it's brushing your teeth, making coffee, or checking emails. Once you have these anchor habits, choose simple, new habits to add to each routine. The key is to start small. You're not trying to overhaul your life overnight; you're making tiny tweaks that add up over time. Tracking progress is important to ensure you're on the right path. Consider using a habit tracker app or a simple checklist. This visual cue is a reminder that provides a sense of accomplishment as you see your progress.

Sticking to habit stacks requires a bit of finesse. Visual cues can be beneficial. Place a sticky note on your coffee maker or set a reminder on your phone. These little nudges keep your new habits top of mind. Celebrating small successes is another crucial element. Give yourself a mental high-five or a small reward each time you complete a habit stack. These celebrations reinforce the behavior, making it more likely to stick. Finally, be open to adjustments. Life isn't static, and neither are your routines. If a habit stack isn't working, tweak it until it fits more comfortably into your life. Maybe the timing is off, or the new habit needs to be smaller. Whatever the case, refining your approach ensures that your habit stacks remain effective and relevant.

STAYING MOTIVATED: CELEBRATING SMALL WINS AND PROGRESS

Imagine setting off on a cross-country road trip without a map or GPS. You know where you want to end up, but every turn becomes a gamble without guidance. Motivation in maintaining organization is your navigation system, guiding you toward your goals with purpose and clarity. Staying motivated helps sustain long-term habits, ensuring your efforts don't fizzle like a firework on a rainy day. Keeping the end goal in sight acts as a compass, guiding your actions and decisions. It reminds you why you started this journey in the first place, encouraging continuous improvement and growth. No matter how small, each step forward is a mile closer to your destination.

Celebrating small wins is like adding fuel to your motivation engine. It keeps you going, even when the road gets bumpy. Creating a reward system for completing tasks can be incredibly effective. Maybe a piece of chocolate for every closet you clean or an episode of your favorite show after a productive afternoon. These rewards act as mini celebrations, acknowledging your hard work and progress. Keeping a journal or log of accomplishments is another powerful tool. It allows you to look back and see how far you've come. Each entry is a testament to your dedication, reminding you that progress is being made, even when it feels like you're standing still. Sharing successes with friends or family can also boost motivation. There's something about the camaraderie of shared victories that makes the process more enjoyable.

The concept of "progress over perfection" is a mantra worth adopting. It emphasizes the importance of focusing on continuous progress rather than achieving a perfect state. Accepting and learning from setbacks is part of the process. It's like learning to ride a bike—you'll wobble and fall, but each attempt brings you closer to mastering the skill. Celebrating incremental improvements, no matter how small, is key. Maybe you didn't organize the entire garage, but you cleared a path to the toolbox. That's progress worth celebrating. Embracing this mindset turns obstacles into stepping stones, helping you move forward with resilience and determination.

Maintaining long-term motivation requires a bit of strategy. Setting new goals and challenges keeps things interesting. It's like adding new destinations to your road trip, ensuring you never tire of the journey. Regularly reviewing and adjusting routines and systems keeps them fresh and relevant. It's about finding what works, tweaking what doesn't, and constantly striving for improvement. Seeking inspiration from books, podcasts, or online communities can reignite your motivation. Sometimes, a new perspective or a shared story is all it takes to rekindle your passion.

As you keep your eyes on the prize, remember that motivation is not a one-time deal. It's a continuous process that requires nurturing and attention. Like a garden, it flourishes with care and wilts with neglect. By celebrating small wins, focusing on progress, and setting new goals, you create a cycle of motivation that propels you forward. You're not just organizing your space; you're crafting a life that reflects your values and aspirations. Each step, each win, brings you closer to a more intentional and fulfilling life.

As we wrap up Chapter 7, remember that motivation is your steadfast companion on this road to organization. It keeps you moving forward, illuminating the path ahead. Now, prepare to shift gears as we explore the emotional and mental well-being aspects of organized living in the upcoming chapter.

8

EMOTIONAL AND MENTAL WELL-BEING

You walk into your living room and find it transformed into a peaceful sanctuary, free from the chaos of scattered magazines and abandoned coffee mugs. Imagine achieving this serenity not through a whirlwind cleaning spree but by embracing a more mindful approach to decluttering. Mindfulness, often associated with meditation, involves being present and fully engaged 'in the moment'. It helps you focus on the task at hand, turning the frequently overwhelming decluttering process into something more manageable and meditative. By concentrating on the present, you reduce anxiety and stress, transforming what could be a chore into an opportunity for mental clarity and calm.

Mindful decluttering is more than just tidying up; it's about actively noticing your surroundings and being aware of your thoughts and feelings as you handle each item. This approach encourages you to be intentional, asking questions like, "What does this item mean to me right now?" or "Does this item serve a current purpose?" Such questions help you determine whether something should stay in your life or make way for something new. If you keep only what sparks joy or adds value to your life, this conscious decision-making process not only aids in decluttering but also aligns your space with your goals and values.

To practice mindfulness while decluttering, start with deep breathing exercises before and during your sessions. Take a few moments to breathe deeply, grounding yourself in the present and calming any swirling thoughts. This simple act can help center your mind, making it easier to focus on the task. As you declutter, create a calm and distraction-free environment. Turn off your phone, play soothing music, and let the outside world disappear. This helps you stay present, allowing you to make thoughtful decisions about each item you touch.

Consider the story of Emma, a busy teacher who found peace through mindful decluttering. Emma had always struggled with letting go of things, often keeping items out of guilt or obligation. But by adopting a conscious approach, she learned to focus on the present value of her belongings. Emma would ask herself, "Does this item improve my life today?" This question became her guiding principle, helping her release what no longer served her. The result was a home that felt lighter and more aligned with her current life, reducing the mental clutter weighing her down.

Another testament to the power of mindfulness in decluttering comes from David, who had a hard time parting with sentimental items. Old birthday cards, concert tickets, and childhood toys cluttered his space, each tied to a precious memory. By practicing mindfulness, David found a new perspective. He realized that the memories and emotions associated with these items remained even without the physical objects. With this understanding, he could let go of some things, keeping only those that truly brought him joy. This shift allowed David to create a living environment that was organized and reflective of his present self.

Interactive Element: Mindful Decluttering Exercise

1. Breathe: Spend a minute focusing on your breath before you start decluttering.
2. Set Your Space: Create a calm environment by minimizing distractions.
3. Reflect: As you handle each item, ask, "Does this add value or joy to my life?"
4. Decide: Keep, donate, or discard based on your reflections.
5. Celebrate: Acknowledge the progress you've made, no matter how small.

Mindful decluttering is a journey toward a more intentional, stress-free life. By embracing mindfulness, you clear physical spaces and free your mind, making room for new experiences and opportunities.

REDUCING STRESS THROUGH ORGANIZATION: CREATING A PEACEFUL ENVIRONMENT

Imagine walking into a room where everything is in its place, like a perfectly orchestrated symphony of calm. The absence of clutter brings an immediate relief, as though you've just stepped into a spa instead of your own home. Clutter doesn't just occupy physical space; it also occupies mental real estate. Visual clutter is like static on a radio, interfering with your ability to think clearly. It competes for your attention, making it difficult to focus on what truly matters. Searching for misplaced items is a daily frustration that can turn even the most patient person into a ball of nerves. Who hasn't felt their blood pressure rise while hunting for car keys when you're already late? This constant state of disorganization leads to anxiety and stress, chipping away at your mental clarity and overall well-being.

Creating a peaceful, organized environment is not just about aesthetics; it's about crafting a refuge from the chaos of everyday life. Start by tackling high-stress areas first. The bedroom and kitchen are prime candidates, spaces where you begin and end your day. Decluttering these areas can have a profound impact on your mental state. Imagine waking up in a bedroom free of laundry piles and cluttered surfaces. It sets a positive tone for the day ahead. Similarly, a tidy kitchen makes meal prep less of a chore and more of a creative outlet. Once you've tackled these spaces, consider the role of decor in crafting a serene atmosphere. Calming colors like soft blues and greens can transform a room into a haven. Introduce noise-reducing elements, like soft fabrics and white noise machines, to enhance tranquility. A plush rug or a few strategically placed cushions can absorb sound, creating a quieter, more peaceful environment.

While organizing, it's easy to get lost in the task at hand. Incorporate relaxation techniques to keep calm and focused during the process. Play soothing music or nature sounds to create an ambient backdrop, making the task feel less like a chore and more like a therapeutic ritual. Take short breaks to practice deep breathing or stretching. It's like hitting the refresh button on your brain, giving you a burst of energy to keep going. These small acts of self-care can make a significant difference in your stress levels and overall organizing experience.

Consider the story of Alex, a busy professional who found calm through an organized workspace. Alex had always struggled with maintaining order at his desk, leading to frantic mornings and misplaced documents. Alex transformed it into a zone of productivity and calm by dedicating time to decluttering and organizing his workspace. Having designated spots for everything—from pens to paperwork—made a world of difference. Alex found that he could focus better with everything in its place, and his stress levels significantly decreased. He even discovered he had more energy and enthusiasm for his work, no longer bogged down by the chaos of disorganization.

Then there's Lisa, a parent who created a more peaceful home environment through decluttering. With kids running around, Lisa's home often felt like a hurricane had swept through. Toys, clothes, and random items were scattered everywhere, making it hard for her to find a moment's peace. By focusing on key areas like the living room and the kids' rooms, Lisa managed to create pockets of calm within the storm. She introduced storage solutions that made tidying up a breeze, even for her little ones. As the clutter diminished, so did her stress, and the entire family benefited from the newfound harmony in their home.

EMOTIONAL ATTACHMENT TO CLUTTER: LETTING GO OF SENTIMENTAL ITEMS

Parting with sentimental items sometimes feels like saying goodbye to an old friend. It's not just a shirt or a piece of furniture—it's a time capsule, a keeper of memories. The quilt your grandma stitched, the ticket stub from your first concert, or your child's first drawing all hold emotional currency. They connect us to moments we cherish and people we miss. But when these items pile up, they can transform our homes into museums of the past, trapping us in nostalgia. The fear of losing these tangible memories can be overwhelming. What if you let go and regret it later? This fear often paralyzes us, making it difficult to part with anything at all.

But here's the thing: while memories are precious, they don't rely on physical objects. There are ways to honor these memories without holding on to every item. Creating a "memory box" can be a gentle way to start. This is your sacred space for those small, meaningful items that truly matter. Knowing you have a designated spot can make it easier to let go of the rest. Another trick is to take photos of items before discarding them. This way, the memory is preserved differently, still accessible whenever you want to reminisce. Writing about the memories associated with certain belongings can also help. Describe how your heart felt when you wore that graduation gown, or remember the laughter shared over a chipped mug. This act of storytelling can be freeing, capturing the essence without needing a physical reminder.

In our quest to declutter, shifting focus from the past to the present and future is key. Ask yourself, "Does this item serve my current life?" If not, it might be time to let go. Instead of clinging to old memories, concentrate on creating new ones. Life is about moving forward; while the past is important, it shouldn't weigh you down. A focus on new experiences can open doors to fresh opportunities and adventures. It's like shedding old skin, making room for growth and renewal.

Take the story of Lucy, who faced a house overflowing with mementos after her parents downsized. Each item seemed laden with history, making it difficult to decide what to keep. She found a balance by creating a memory box and snapping photos of larger items. Lucy discovered freedom in letting go of the excess, keeping only those things that brought her the most joy. She realized her memories were in her heart, not just the objects. Then there's Tom, who downsized from a large family home to a cozy apartment. Faced with the challenge of limited space, he had to be selective. Tom focused on keeping items aligned with his current lifestyle, finding solace in the simplicity of a clutter-free environment. The sentimental items he retained truly enriched his life, not just cluttered his space.

Letting go of sentimental items isn't about erasing the past. It's about honoring it while making room for the present. It's about choosing to cherish what's meaningful and releasing what's not, knowing the memories live on in your heart. Life is a continuous growth journey, and sometimes, that means learning to let go.

AFFIRMATIONS AND POSITIVE REINFORCEMENT: ENCOURAGING YOURSELF

Picture the scene: you're standing in the middle of your living room, surrounded by piles of things you swear you've never seen before, wondering how in the world it got this bad. It's like your clutter has started its own, little revolution. Enter affirmations and positive reinforcement—more weapons in your decluttering arsenal. Affirmations are like little pep talks you give yourself; they can boost your motivation and confidence when you feel like giving up. They work by reinforcing positive beliefs and attitudes, helping you shift your mindset from "I can't do this" to "I am nailing this." The psychological benefits of affirmations are well-documented. They can reduce stress, increase optimism, and improve your overall well-being. You're essentially rewiring your brain to adopt a more constructive outlook by repeating positive statements. And when it comes to decluttering, this can make all the difference.

Positive reinforcement takes this a step further by rewarding yourself for making progress, no matter how small. Think of it as giving yourself a gold star for every drawer you organize or every item you donate. This kind of reinforcement creates lasting behavioral changes by associating positive feelings with the act of decluttering. It's like training your dog to sit by giving them a treat—only in this case, you're the dog, and the treat might be a cup of hot coffee or an episode of your favorite show. By consistently rewarding your efforts, you build a habit of decluttering that feels less like a chore and more like an act of self-care.

Now, let's arm you with some affirmations to help you stay on track. Start with, "I can create a peaceful and organized space." This affirmation reminds you that you have the power to transform your environment. Another favorite is, "Letting go of clutter brings clarity and calm to my life." It reinforces the idea that decluttering isn't about losing something; it's about gaining space, both physically and mentally. Lastly, try, "Each small step I take leads to a more organized home." This one is all about progress over perfection, encouraging you to celebrate every victory, no matter how tiny.

Incorporating affirmations into your daily routine can be as simple as repeating them during your morning or evening rituals. You might say them out loud or even whisper them to yourself as you enjoy your morning coffee. Writing them on sticky notes and placing them around your home can also serve as gentle reminders throughout the day. You could stick one on your bathroom mirror, another on the fridge, and one on your nightstand. Affirmation apps and recordings are available for those who prefer digital reminders. These tools can provide a daily dose of encouragement right from your smartphone.

Consider Jane, a reader who found renewed motivation through positive reinforcement. Jane had always struggled with maintaining an organized home, feeling overwhelmed by the sheer amount of stuff she'd accumulated over the years. By using affirmations, she shifted her mindset from one of defeat to one of empowerment. Whenever she tackled a small area, she rewarded herself with a little treat—a walk in the park, a favorite snack. Over time, these small acts of self-kindness added up, and Jane found herself not only with a more organized home but also with a more positive outlook on life.

Then there's Tom, who used affirmations to overcome his decluttering challenges. Tom was initially skeptical, but he decided to give it a try. He repeated his chosen affirmations daily, focusing on his progress rather than the mountains of clutter still left to tackle. Slowly but surely, his perspective began to change. He started to see his home not as a lost cause but as a work in progress. With each step forward, Tom gained confidence, and what once felt impossible became achievable.

Affirmations and positive reinforcement are powerful tools that can transform your decluttering journey. They remind you that you are capable, that progress is worth celebrating, and that you deserve to live in a space that reflects your best self. So, permit yourself to embrace these techniques. Speak kindly to yourself, reward your efforts, and watch as your home and mindset begin to change for the better.

As we close this chapter, remember that the road to a clutter-free life is paved with small steps and self-compassion. Next, we'll explore the tools and resources to make this road smoother and help you maintain your newfound sense of order and peace.

9
TOOLS AND RESOURCES

Ever wonder why some days feel like you're juggling swords while walking a tightrope? You're not alone. Many adults with ADHD find themselves in a whirlwind of tasks, trying to keep everything from crashing down. But fear not—there's a tool that can help bring order to the chaos: the humble checklist. Picture it as your trusty companion, ready to catch those runaway tasks before they slip through the cracks. Checklists and worksheets are more than just to-do lists; they're lifelines. They provide structure and clarity, transforming overwhelming tasks into manageable steps. Think of them as maps guiding you through the labyrinth of daily life, ensuring you don't miss a turn.

Checklists are incredibly effective, especially for adults with ADHD, who often benefit from structured environments. According to Psychology Today, simple tools like checklists can help maintain focus across different age groups. When you visualize tasks and break them down into bite-sized pieces, the sense of achievement grows with every item checked off. It's like leveling up in a video game—you gain momentum and confidence with each completed task. Whether it's a daily chore list, a weekly cleaning schedule, or a comprehensive project plan, checklists provide a tangible sense of progress and accomplishment.

Let's delve into some examples of how checklists can be used effectively. Daily and weekly task checklists manage routine activities and ensure nothing slips through the cracks. Picture this: a list that greets you every morning, ready to guide your day with tasks neatly lined up, offering the satisfaction of ticking them off one at a time. Decluttering worksheets can help you tackle your home, room by room, ensuring no clutter monster is left lurking in the shadows. Maintenance schedules are perfect for those recurring chores—think cleaning routines or plant-watering schedules. And for those big dreams and goals? SMART goal-setting worksheets are your go-to, turning vague aspirations into concrete, actionable steps.

But how do you make these tools work for you? The key lies in customization. Tailor your checklists to fit your unique needs and preferences. Add personalized categories to keep everything organized—maybe separate your work tasks from your to-dos. Color-coding can be a game-changer, visually distinguishing between different types of tasks and making your list a vibrant roadmap. Don't forget to leave space for notes and reflections, allowing you to jot down thoughts or adjustments as you go. These tweaks transform checklists from generic templates into personalized guides that resonate with your lifestyle.

In today's digital age, you have many options at your fingertips. Websites and apps offer a treasure trove of printable templates, perfect for those who enjoy the tactile satisfaction of pen and paper. But if digital is more your style, tools like Microsoft To-Do or Google Keep offer the flexibility to create and manage lists on the go. They're great for syncing across devices, ensuring your checklist is always a tap away. For those who prefer a more hands-on approach, creating custom checklists using word processors or spreadsheet software allows for endless possibilities. You can design your perfect checklist with all the bells and whistles that suit your organizational style.

Interactive Element: Create Your Custom Checklist

- Identify Tasks: Write down all the tasks you need to accomplish. Categorize them by type (e.g., home, work, personal).
- Customize: Add categories, color-code tasks, and leave space for notes.
- Choose Your Format: Decide if you prefer a printable version or a digital tool like Microsoft To-Do.
- Reflect: After using your checklist for a week, reflect on its effectiveness and make the necessary adjustments.

Armed with these tools, you will be ready to tackle the turmoil and turn your juggling act into a well-choreographed dance. Embrace the power of checklists and worksheets, and watch as they help you transform chaos into calm.

USING PLANNERS AND BULLET JOURNALS: CUSTOMIZING YOUR SYSTEM

Picture your life as a symphony of tasks, plans, and dreams all playing simultaneously. To conduct this orchestra, you need a tool capable of handling the chaos and bringing harmony to your daily routine. Enter planners and bullet journals—the maestros of the organization. These tools are more than calendars; they're like your personal assistants, helping manage time, set goals, and track progress. Imagine having a single place where your task lists, schedules, and notes coexist peacefully, each supporting the other. This integration encourages regular reflection and planning, allowing you to see the big picture while focusing on the most important details.

Choosing the right planner or bullet journal needs a little contemplation. Traditional planners offer structure and predictability with their weekly and monthly layouts. They're perfect for those who thrive on routine and appreciate the tactile satisfaction of pen on paper. Then there are bullet journals, the customizable, flexible format allowing creativity and personalization. Bullet journaling is like having a blank canvas where you get to design the system that works best for you, adapting as your needs change. If you're a tech enthusiast, digital planners might be your go-to. These apps and software bring planning on the go, syncing across devices and offering features that physical planners can't match, like reminders and notifications.

Now, once you've picked your tool of choice, it's time to make it your own. Creating a bullet journal? Start by making an index and key. These elements are your navigation guide, helping you quickly find and interpret your entries. Add a splash of personality with stickers or other decorative elements. This isn't just for aesthetics; it's about making your planner an engaging space. Incorporate habit trackers and goal-setting pages to keep tabs on your progress and stay motivated. Consider adding sections for specific projects or areas of focus, ensuring everything you need is at your fingertips when you need it.

The internet is a treasure trove of ideas for those seeking inspiration. YouTube channels and blogs dedicated to bullet journaling abound, offering tutorials and walkthroughs that can spark your creativity. Online communities and forums are great spaces to connect with fellow planner enthusiasts, share tips, and gain insights into different styles and techniques. Books and courses on effective planning and journaling techniques can also provide structured guidance, helping you refine your approach and make the most of these powerful tools.

The beauty of planners and bullet journals lies in their ability to adapt to your life. As your priorities shift and evolve, so too can your system. Whether scheduling meetings, setting personal goals, or tracking daily habits, these tools offer a customizable solution that grows with you. They're not about rigid rules or one-size-fits-all solutions—they're about finding what works for you and embracing the journey of self-discovery and organization. So, grab your planner or bullet journal and start crafting a system that organizes your life and inspires and empowers you every step of the way.

APPS AND DIGITAL TOOLS: LEVERAGING TECHNOLOGY FOR ORGANIZATION

Imagine having a personal assistant at your fingertips, ready to remind you of tasks, organize your thoughts, and even help you collaborate with others. That's the magic of apps and digital tools—they're not just software but allies in your quest for organization. These tools help centralize all your tasks and information, ensuring everything you need is in one accessible place. No more sticky notes scattered around like confetti after a party or trying to remember where you saved that important file. Apps provide reminders and notifications, acting like a gentle nudge when you're about to forget a deadline or a meeting. It's like having a friend who's always got your back, ensuring you stay on top of things. Plus, they enable collaboration and sharing, so everyone stays in the loop whether you're planning a project with a team or a family event.

When choosing the right digital tools, the options are as varied as toppings at a pizza parlor. Task management apps like Trello, Asana, and Todoist are great for organizing tasks and projects, allowing you to break down big tasks into smaller, manageable steps. They are digital sticky notes that won't get lost under your couch cushions. Calendar and scheduling apps like Google Calendar and Microsoft Outlook ensure you never miss an appointment. They sync across devices, so your schedule is always at your fingertips whether you're on your computer or phone. Note-taking apps such as Evernote and OneNote are perfect for capturing ideas and information, offering a virtual notebook that's as organized as needed. For keeping track of habits and routines, apps like Habitica and Streaks turn habit-building into a game, making developing new, productive routines fun.

Choosing the right app can feel like picking a new pair of shoes—it must fit just right. Start by considering user-friendliness and ease of use; you want a tool that feels natural, not like learning a new language. Compatibility with other tools and devices is crucial—your app should play nicely with your existing digital palette. Look for features and functionalities that match your specific needs, whether it's reminders, task prioritization, or collaboration options. Also, consider the availability of free versus premium versions. Many apps offer basic features for free, with premium options for those who need extra firepower.

Once you've chosen your arsenal of apps, it's time to integrate them into your life. Syncing apps across multiple devices ensures you have access to your information no matter where you are. Set up notifications and reminders to keep important tasks front and center. Regularly update and review tasks and information to keep everything current and relevant. This is where digital tools shine—they offer flexibility and adaptability, allowing you to adjust as your needs change. Don't be afraid to use apps with physical tools like planners and notebooks. Combining digital and physical systems can provide the best of both worlds, offering tactile satisfaction and digital efficiency.

In this tech-savvy age, embracing digital tools for organizations can transform how you manage your life. They offer structure and support, turning chaos into clarity. The key is finding the right combination that fits your unique lifestyle and using it naturally and effectively. Whether managing a busy work schedule or trying to keep track of personal goals, these apps are like having a team of experts at your fingertips, ready to assist whenever you need them.

SUPPORT NETWORKS: FINDING HELP AND ENCOURAGEMENT

Picture yourself as a lone sailor navigating the stormy seas of life with ADHD. It can feel isolating like you're the only one battling the waves of distraction and disorganization. This is where a support network becomes invaluable. Connecting with others who understand your challenges can provide the motivation, accountability, and encouragement you need to keep your ship steady. A strong support network can reduce feelings of isolation and overwhelm, offering a safe harbor where you can share tips, advice, and experiences. It's about finding your crew, those who will help you stay on course and weather any storm that comes your way.

Several types of support networks can be incredibly beneficial for adults with ADHD. Online forums and social media groups dedicated to ADHD and organization are great places to start. They offer a platform for sharing experiences and solutions with people who truly get it. Local support groups and meetups provide face-to-face interaction, which can be incredibly affirming and empowering. You can also consider professional organizers and coaches who specialize in ADHD. They bring expertise and personalized strategies to the table, helping you tackle your unique challenges head-on. And let's not forget the role of friends and family members who understand and support your goals. They are your cheerleaders, always ready to celebrate your victories, big or small.

Building and maintaining a strong support network requires effort, but it is always worth it. Start by reaching out to existing contacts and communities. You might find that friends or colleagues are already part of supportive groups you can join. Online platforms are a fantastic resource. Participate in discussions, ask questions, and share your insights. You'll find that many people are eager to connect and lend support. Attending local events and workshops is another great way to meet like-minded individuals and expand your network. Don't hesitate to seek professional support when needed. Coaches and therapists who specialize in ADHD can offer tailored advice and strategies, helping you navigate challenges with confidence.

Finding the right support network isn't a one-size-fits-all process. It's about exploring different options and discovering what resonates with you. Websites and directories are a good starting point for locating local support groups. Social media platforms and hashtags can connect you with online communities that fit your interests and needs. Look into professional associations for organizers and coaches, as they often have directories of qualified professionals. Online courses and webinars can also be valuable, offering insights into building effective support networks. The trick is to stay open and proactive, seeking opportunities to connect and collaborate.

As you build your support network, remember that it's not just about receiving help—it's about giving it too. Share your own experiences and insights, offering encouragement to others who are on a similar path. This reciprocity strengthens connections and creates a sense of community where everyone feels valued and supported. Your network becomes a source of strength, helping you stay grounded and focused no matter your challenges. So, set sail with your newfound crew, knowing you're not alone on this journey.

In the next chapter, we'll explore how to involve friends and family in organizing efforts, turning them into allies in your quest for a more intentional life. This is where the magic happens—when your personal support system aligns with your organizational goals, creating a harmonious and supportive environment that fosters growth and success.

10
INVOLVING FAMILY AND FRIENDS

Have you ever felt like you're the only one holding the broom in a house full of chaos? You're trying to create harmony, but everyone else seems to be dancing to a different tune. Organizing your home can be a Herculean task, especially when it feels like you're the only one who notices the trail of socks leading from the living room to the kitchen. But what if you could recruit your family members and friends to join your squad? Imagine transforming your space with a bit of help from your nearest and dearest, turning what feels like a solo struggle into a team triumph.

COMMUNICATING YOUR NEEDS: HOW TO ASK FOR HELP

Clear communication is the backbone of any successful team, including your home organization squad. When you're asking for help, setting the right tone for the conversation is essential. Picture it like inviting someone to join a treasure hunt rather than asking them to shovel snow. You want to make it sound like an opportunity, not a burden. Be specific about the type of help you need. Instead of saying, "I need help organizing," try, "Could you help me sort through the kids' toys on Saturday?" This way, you're giving them a straightforward task with a defined time, making it easier for them to say yes.

Use "I" statements to convey your feelings when expressing your needs. This approach can help prevent defensiveness and open the door to a more productive dialogue. Instead of saying, "You never help with the cleaning," rephrase it to, "I feel overwhelmed managing all the cleaning on my own." This subtle shift in language can make a world of difference. Avoid blame or criticism, as these can quickly derail a conversation. Focus on being clear and concise about what you need help with, whether tackling that ever-growing pile of laundry or decluttering the garage.

Timing and setting matter, too. Choose an appropriate moment to have your conversation. Maybe wait until after dinner, when everyone is more relaxed and receptive. Avoid mentioning it when tensions are high or someone is rushing out the door. Preparing a list of tasks or areas you need help can also be beneficial. It gives the other person a clear understanding of the agenda and allows for better planning. Be open to feedback and suggestions. Your family or friends might have ideas or preferences that could make the process more enjoyable or efficient for everyone involved.

Let me share a story about a couple I know, Sam and Alex, who turned their home from shame to serene through open dialogue. They started by having a heart-to-heart about how the clutter was affecting their lives. Sam felt overwhelmed by the disarray, while Alex was frustrated by the nagging. By using "I" statements, they could express their feelings without pointing fingers. They agreed to tackle one room at a time, starting with the kitchen. Alex took charge of decluttering the pantry while Sam focused on organizing the cabinets. By setting specific tasks and supporting each other, they transformed their kitchen into a functional space and strengthened their relationship.

Then there's Emily, a parent who successfully involved her children in decluttering. She realized her kids were more likely to participate if they felt included in decision-making. Emily organized a family meeting where everyone had a say in which toys to keep and which to donate. By empowering her children to make choices, she got their buy-in and taught them valuable organizational skills. The result? A tidier home and kids who felt proud of their contribution to the family's well-being.

Interactive Exercise: Crafting Your Communication Plan

1. Identify Your Needs: List specific tasks where you'd like help.
2. Choose Your Words Wisely: Practice using "I" statements to express your needs.
3. Plan the Conversation: Select an appropriate time and setting to discuss your needs.
4. Prepare for Feedback: Be open to suggestions and willing to adjust your plan.

Communicating your needs doesn't have to be daunting. Setting the right tone and being clear and specific can turn what might feel like a solo effort into a team victory. And remember, it's not just about getting help; it's about building stronger connections and fostering a supportive environment.

ORGANIZING AS A FAMILY: COLLABORATIVE STRATEGIES

Think of your home as an art project, where every family member holds a brush and a vision. When everyone pitches in, organizing can become more than just tidying up. It becomes a shared experience, a canvas where cooperation and teamwork flourish. Working together strengthens family bonds and makes the process enjoyable and rewarding. You're not just sorting through old magazines or decluttering the attic; you're building a narrative of collaboration and mutual achievement. Each member plays a part, creating a harmonious living space that reflects the collective effort.

The beauty of organizing as a family lies in tailoring tasks to individual strengths and preferences. If Dad has a knack for assembling furniture, let him tackle the garage shelves. If your teenager loves music, hand them the task of creating a playlist for organizing sessions. Even the little ones can join in, sorting toys by color or shape. This division of labor ensures everyone feels involved and valued, turning a potentially mundane chore into an engaging activity. Setting up family organizing sessions with clear goals can further enhance this experience. Think of it as setting the stage for a play, where each act has a purpose, and everyone knows their role. You could aim to transform the living room into a clutter-free zone or revamp the kitchen pantry to make it more functional. Whatever the goal, clarity ensures everyone is on the same page.

Injecting some fun into the mix can make organizing less of a task and more of a game. Consider using challenges or competitions to spark enthusiasm. Who can sort through their closet the fastest? Which team can create the tidiest bookshelf? Adding a playful element boosts motivation and makes the time pass more quickly. These games can turn a dreary afternoon into a lively event, with laughter and a sense of accomplishment.

Keeping family members engaged over time requires a blend of strategy and creativity. Regular family meetings to discuss progress can keep everyone on track and informed. They offer a platform for celebrating successes and addressing any hiccups. A reward system for completed tasks can also work wonders. Perhaps a movie night or a special dinner out for a job well done? Such incentives not only motivate but also serve as a reminder that hard work pays off. Open communication and feedback are equally vital. Encourage each member to voice their thoughts and ideas, creating an inclusive environment where everyone's input is valued.

Take the Lopez family, for example. They turned their cluttered living room into a cozy retreat by working together. Each family member had a role: Mom sorted through books, Dad tackled the tangled mess of cables behind the TV, and their kids organized board games and DVDs. The transformation was stunning, but what they cherished most was the time spent together, laughing and sharing stories as they worked. Similarly, the Parkers, two parents with energetic kids, faced the daunting task of organizing their chaotic garage. By involving their children in sorting tools and sports equipment, they got the job done, and their kids learned valuable lessons in teamwork and responsibility.

Organizing as a family is more than just decluttering; it's about weaving together the threads of cooperation, fun, and communication. The physical transformation of your home is just one part of the equation. The real magic happens in the connections you strengthen and the memories you create.

TEACHING KIDS ORGANIZATIONAL SKILLS: SETTING UP FOR SUCCESS

Visualize a child's room where toys are neatly stored, books are lined up like soldiers ready for inspection, and clothes are folded, not strewn about like a tornado just passed through. Sound like a dream? It doesn't have to be. Teaching kids organizational skills is not just about maintaining a tidy room—it's about instilling habits that will benefit them throughout their lives. When kids learn to organize, they develop responsibility and independence. They start to understand the importance of caring for their belongings and managing their space, which fosters a sense of pride and ownership. Moreover, creating a sense of order and routine helps them feel secure and confident, knowing there's a place for everything and everything is in its place.

So, how do you make organization fun and engaging for kids? Start by using age-appropriate tasks and language. For younger children, simple tasks like sorting toys by color or size can be educational and enjoyable. Older kids can handle more complex tasks, such as organizing their study space or planning their weekly schedule. The key is incorporating organization into daily routines, making it as natural as brushing their teeth or putting on their pajamas. Encourage them to tidy up before bedtime or after playtime, turning it into a game rather than a chore. Modeling organized behavior is crucial, too. Kids are like sponges, absorbing everything around them. They'll be more likely to follow suit when they see you organizing your space and staying on top of tasks.

Plenty of tools and resources help teach kids the ropes of organization. Checklists and chore charts are fantastic for tracking tasks and providing a visual reminder of what needs to be done. You can even let your kids decorate their charts, adding a personal touch that makes them more invested. There are also organizational games and activities designed to teach these skills playfully. Whether it's a board game that requires sorting or a digital app that simulates real-life scenarios, these tools can make learning fun. Books and resources on organization for kids are another excellent way to introduce these concepts. Stories featuring characters who learn to organize can provide entertainment and valuable lessons.

I remember Jane's story, a parent who used a chore chart to teach her child the importance of organization. Jane's daughter, Emma, was initially resistant to tidying up her toys. However, once Jane introduced a colorful chore chart with stickers as a reward, Emma found value in this and enjoyed the activity. She'd add a sticker to her chart each time she completed a task. The visual representation of her accomplishments motivated Emma, and over time, she began to take pride in keeping her room tidy. Jane found that this simple hack helped Emma stay organized and taught her about responsibility and following through on tasks.

In another example, Mr. Thomson, an elementary school teacher, incorporated organizational skills into his classroom. He noticed that his students often struggled to keep their desks tidy and their assignments in order. To address this, he introduced a "desk detective" game, where students would pretend to be detectives searching for clues (in this case, their supplies and papers). Each week, a student with the tidiest desk would win the title "Top Detective" and receive a small reward. The game encouraged friendly competition and instilled a sense of pride in maintaining a neat workspace. Mr. Thomson found that his students became more organized, translating into better focus and performance in class.

Teaching kids organizational skills is a gift that keeps on giving. It's not just about keeping their space tidy; it's about setting them up for success in all areas of life. With the right strategies, tools, and encouragement, you can help your kids develop habits that will serve them well into adulthood.

MANAGING CONFLICT: NAVIGATING DIFFERENCES IN ORGANIZATIONAL STYLES

Living with others can sometimes feel like you're trying to solve a puzzle where the pieces are constantly shifting. You might adore a minimalist look, while your roommate sees nothing wrong with a dozen knick-knacks on every surface. It's not just about aesthetics; it's about different tolerance levels for clutter and varying approaches to tidiness. One person's cozy might be another's chaos. These differences can lead to disagreements and tension, especially if expectations aren't communicated. When trying to create a harmonious living space, it's crucial to recognize these divergent styles and address them head-on. Otherwise, you could be in a constant tug-of-war, where no one truly feels at home.

Managing these conflicts starts with practicing active listening and empathy. Instead of focusing solely on your perspective, understand where the other person is coming from. Why do they prefer their way of organizing? What does a tidy space mean to them? You can uncover the underlying reasons behind their preferences by showing empathy and genuinely listening. This opens the door to finding common ground and compromise. You can find agreement in a shared area like the living room, keeping it tidy while allowing for more personal freedom in private spaces. It's all about balance and ensuring everyone feels comfortable in their home.

Setting clear boundaries and expectations is another vital strategy. If you share a space with someone more relaxed about clutter, it's crucial to establish what's acceptable and what's not. You might agree to keep the common areas tidy while allowing individual rooms to reflect personal styles. Having these boundaries in place helps prevent misunderstandings and resentment. It creates a framework where everyone can express their individuality without encroaching on each other's space.

Creating a harmonious environment involves more than just compromise. It's about respecting individual preferences and spaces and acknowledging that everyone has their way of doing things. Encouraging open and respectful communication is key. Make it a habit to check in with each other, discussing how the current setup is working and what might need tweaking. This ongoing dialogue ensures that everyone feels heard and valued, fostering cooperation and reducing the likelihood of conflict.

Take the example of Sarah and Mark, a couple who found themselves constantly clashing over their different organizational styles. Sarah loved a spotless home, while Mark was more laid-back. By sitting down and discussing their needs and preferences, they discovered that Sarah's desire for cleanliness stemmed from a need for control, while Mark's relaxed approach was rooted in a passion for comfort. They compromised by maintaining a neat living room and allowing for more flexibility in personal spaces. This understanding and compromise transformed their home from a battleground into a sanctuary for both.

Then there's the story of Kathy and Mike, roommates who initially struggled to tidy their shared apartment. Kathy was a neat freak, while Mike was more of a free spirit. They decided to establish a cleaning schedule and divided responsibilities based on what each was good at—Kathy handled the kitchen and bathroom, while Mike took charge of the living room and hallway. This division of labor and regular check-ins helped them maintain a tidy space and strengthened their friendship.

As you navigate the complexities of shared living spaces, remember that conflict is not the enemy. It's an opportunity for growth and understanding. By approaching differences with empathy, setting clear boundaries, and fostering open communication, you can create a home where everyone feels respected and valued. In the next chapter, we'll explore the unique circumstances that require particular organizational strategies, such as living in small spaces and managing unexpected life events.

II
SPECIAL CIRCUMSTANCES

There you are, standing in your tiny studio apartment, surrounded by piles of stuff that seem to have a life of their own. Your kitchen table doubles as your office, bed, and sometimes your dining room. You have more things than space and no magic wand to make it all disappear. If you've ever found yourself in such a space, you know exactly how challenging it is to keep things organized. The limited square footage can feel like it's closing in on you, turning what should be a cozy nook into a claustrophobic nightmare. Visual clutter becomes your constant, unwanted roommate, and every inch of space is premium real estate.

One major hurdle in small spaces is the glaring lack of storage options. It's like trying to fit a giraffe into a Mini Cooper. You open a closet, and it's already bursting at the seams, laughing at your attempt to squeeze in just one more pair of shoes. Then there's the issue of multipurpose rooms —when your living room is also your bedroom, office, and gym, finding a way to organize without it looking like a yard sale is tough. And let's not forget visual clutter. In compact environments, even a few scattered items can make the place look like a tornado hit it.

But don't lose hope yet—there are clever tricks to make the most of your limited space. Vertical storage solutions are a game-changer. Wall-mounted shelves and pegboards can turn your walls into valuable storage areas, freeing up floor space. Think of it as giving your floors a little breathing room. Multi-functional furniture is another lifesaver. A storage ottoman can hide your clutter while doubling as a coffee table or extra seating. Sofa beds, storage benches, and tables with built-in storage are fantastic ways to maximize utility without sacrificing style. And let's not overlook the space under your bed, which can become a treasure trove of storage with the suitable containers. It's like having a secret attic, minus the cobwebs.

The backs of doors and cabinets often go unnoticed, offering prime storage opportunities. Over-the-door racks for shoes or pantry items can free up significant space elsewhere. And if you're feeling a bit daring, consider using hooks or magnetic strips inside cabinet doors for small items like spices or cleaning supplies. It's like adding a secret storage spot that only you know about.

Minimalism is your best friend when it comes to small spaces. It's about assessing the necessity of each item and embracing quality over quantity. Do you need three spatulas, or are you just preparing for an impromptu pancake marathon? The "one-in, one-out" rule can also help maintain balance. For every new item you bring in, let go of something old. It's a refreshing way to keep clutter at bay and ensure your space only holds what you truly need and love.

Take, for instance, Jane, who turned her cramped studio apartment into a tidy haven. She created more room and a streamlined look in her closet by installing floating shelves and opting for slim, non-slip hangers. Her kitchen became a model of efficiency with wall-mounted racks for pots and pans. Then there's the Garcia family, who transformed their tiny home into a well-organized space using creative storage solutions like wicker baskets and tiered carts. They found ways to make every nook and cranny functional, proving that even the smallest homes can hold big dreams. Lastly, there's Mark, a professional who turned his compact home office into a powerhouse of productivity by doubling his closet space with two hanging rails and utilizing every inch of space above his cabinets.

Interactive Exercise: Your Small Space Action Plan

Grab a notepad and walk around your space. Identify three areas where you can implement vertical storage. Consider one piece of multi-functional furniture that could improve your space. Try to adopt the "one-in, one-out" rule for a month, and note the changes.

These examples show that small spaces can be functional and inviting with a bit of creativity and strategic planning. You don't need to live in a mansion to create a home that feels spacious and organized. Remember, it's not about the space size but how you use it.

MOVING AND RELOCATION: STAYING ORGANIZED THROUGH TRANSITIONS

So, you're gearing up for a move. Exciting, right? New beginnings, fresh starts, and all that jazz. But let's be real for a second—moving can feel like you're trying to juggle flaming pineapples while riding a unicycle. The stress and disorganization of packing up your life and relocating to a new space can be overwhelming. You've got boxes in every corner, a mountain of packing tape, and a growing sense of dread about how you'll ever find your favorite mug again. Transitioning to a new place brings its own set of challenges. You're not just moving stuff; you're moving memories, routines, and the comfort of the familiar.

Packing and unpacking are like the yin and yang of moving—two forces that seem forever intertwined. Packing your belongings means playing the ultimate game of Tetris, trying to fit every odd-shaped item into a box that appears just a bit too small. Unpacking, on the other hand, is like a scavenger hunt, only the treasure is buried under layers of bubble wrap and misplaced labels. Managing logistics and timelines adds another layer of complexity. From coordinating moving trucks to juggling utility setups, it's easy to feel buried under an avalanche of tasks.

But fear not, for a little organization can go a long way. Start by creating a moving checklist and timeline. This is your roadmap through the chaos. Include everything from booking movers to notifying your grandma of your new address. Breaking tasks into manageable steps makes the whole process feel less like climbing Everest and more like a stroll. Decluttering before packing is a sanity saver. Sort your items into categories like keep, donate, sell, and discard. It's like spring cleaning on steroids, ensuring you only take what you truly need and love to your new home.

Labeling boxes is a game-changer. Think of it as writing a love letter to your future self—one that saves you from tearing through every box just to find a spatula. Keep an inventory of what's in each box. This way, when someone inevitably asks, "Where's my favorite sweater?" you'll have an answer that doesn't involve a wild goose chase. Once you arrive at your new place, set up essential items first. Nothing says "home," like a made bed and a functional bathroom. The little things make a big difference when you're knee-deep in cardboard.

Once the dust settles and the movers have left, it's time to maintain that organization post-move. Unpack one room at a time. Trying to tackle everything at once is a surefire way to drive yourself bananas. Focus on one area, set it up, and then move on to the next. Implementing organizational systems in your new space sets the tone for a clutter-free life. Regularly review and adjust your setup. What works on day one might need tweaking by day thirty, and that's perfectly okay.

Take Amanda, for example, a professional who recently relocated for work. She managed to stay organized by creating a detailed moving plan and sticking to it like glue. Her secret? She labeled boxes with the room and the contents, making unpacking a breeze. Then there's the Rodriguez family, who moved to a new city and maintained order by setting up their new home one room at a time. They found that focusing on immediate essentials helped them settle in without feeling overwhelmed. And let's not forget Jim, who downsized to a smaller home. He embraced minimalism and used the move as an opportunity to shed unnecessary items, creating a space that feels curated and intentional.

Moving doesn't have to be a nightmare of epic proportions. With careful planning and a touch of humor, you can navigate the chaos and emerge on the other side with your sanity intact. Remember what we discussed before, it's about progress, not perfection.

SEASONAL ORGANIZATION: PREPARING FOR HOLIDAYS AND CHANGES

Picture this: it's the first chilly autumn morning, and you're rummaging through your closet, desperately hunting for that cozy sweater you're sure you have—somewhere. Meanwhile, last year's holiday decorations are scattered in the attic, a tangled mess that looks more like a spider's web than a festive display. Sound familiar? Seasonal transitions can often feel like a whirlwind, leaving you frazzled and stressed. But with a pinch of preparation, you can turn these transitions into a smooth ride. You can reduce stress and amplify enjoyment by managing seasonal clothing and decor, planning for holiday events, and adjusting routines. It's about making the most of each season without the chaos, so you can focus on what truly matters, like sipping hot cocoa by the fireplace.

Organizing seasonal items is like setting up a backstage crew for your life's theatrical production. Labeled bins and containers are your stagehands, keeping everything from holiday lights to Halloween costumes in their designated spots. By clearly labeling these bins, you'll save yourself the annual headache of digging through boxes labeled "miscellaneous". Rotating seasonal clothing in and out of storage is another game-changer. You don't need your winter coat taking up precious closet space in July. Keep it tucked away until the frost returns and your closet will thank you. A dedicated system for seasonal sports equipment and outdoor gear is essential for those with a penchant for outdoor adventures. Whether it's snowboards or surfboards, having a designated spot for these items keeps your space tidy and your mind at ease.

Enter the seasonal organization calendar, your new best friend in the quest for a stress-free year. This calendar isn't just for birthdays and dentist appointments. It's your secret weapon for scheduling specific times for decorating and undecorating, ensuring that your home transitions seamlessly from pumpkin patches to winter wonderlands. Consider setting reminders for seasonal maintenance tasks like HVAC checks or garden prep. These little nudges help you stay on top of things without the frantic last-minute scramble. And let's not forget holiday shopping and cooking. Planning ahead means you can savor these moments instead of turning into a frazzled whirlwind of wrapping paper and flour.

Consider the Smith family, who transformed their holiday chaos into a well-oiled machine. By streamlining their preparations and sticking to a calendar, they enjoyed more quality family time rather than battling tangled lights. They even managed to turn decorating into a fun annual tradition, complete with hot cocoa and holiday music. Then, Emily tackled her seasonal wardrobe changes like a pro. She avoided the dreaded closet explosion by setting aside a weekend each season to swap out clothes. Her mornings went from frantic searches to peaceful outfit selections. And let's not forget about Gary, who implemented a seasonal maintenance routine that made his home feel like a sanctuary. By scheduling tasks like gutter cleaning and garden prep, he ensured his house was always ready for whatever Mother Nature threw his way.

Interactive Element: Create Your Seasonal Calendar

Grab a calendar and jot down vital seasonal tasks. Include reminders for decorating, maintenance, and even a few fun activities. Block out time for holiday shopping and cooking, and watch your stress levels drop as your organization skyrockets.

HANDLING UNEXPECTED LIFE EVENTS: STAYING ORGANIZED DURING CRISES

Life has a way of throwing curveballs when you least expect them. One minute, everything's humming smoothly, and the next, you're dealing with a health emergency, a sudden job loss, or a natural disaster that turns your world upside down. It's as if the universe decided you needed a little excitement and not the good kind. These unexpected life events can disrupt the organizational systems you've worked so hard to implement. You might find yourself wading through piles of paperwork or scrambling to find that important document you swear you filed away safely. The moment's chaos can quickly spill over into your physical space, making an already stressful situation even more challenging to manage.

During such times, the first step is acknowledging that maintaining perfect order is a tall order in the face of chaos. But fear not because there are ways to keep your head above water. Creating emergency kits and plans is one such lifesaver. Think of it as prepping your lifeboat before the storm hits. Whether it's a grab-and-go bag for a health crisis or a well-stocked emergency kit for natural disasters, having these essentials ready can save you valuable time and energy when needed. Establishing a central location for important documents and information is another savvy strategy. This could be a physical folder or a digital file on your computer—whatever works best for you. Having all your crucial information in one place means you won't be tearing the house apart looking for that elusive insurance policy or birth certificate.

In our digital age, leveraging technology for organizations is a no-brainer. Use digital tools to back up and access critical information. Cloud services, for example, offer a safety net for your important documents, ensuring they're accessible even if your physical copies are lost or damaged. It's like having a digital vault that keeps your vital information safe and sound. You can also explore apps that help manage tasks and appointments, which can be particularly helpful when your mental bandwidth is stretched thin.

Flexibility and adaptability are your best allies in navigating these turbulent waters. Sometimes, you need to prioritize essential tasks and temporarily shelve the non-essentials. It's okay to let go of your usual routines if they no longer serve you in the current situation. Seek support from family, friends, or professionals when needed. Remember, you don't have to go through the storm alone. Adjust your routines to fit the new circumstances, and don't be afraid to ask for help. It's not a sign of weakness but a testament to your resourcefulness and resilience.

Consider the story of Stepanie, who faced a health crisis that turned her world topsy-turvy. Despite the upheaval, she managed to stay organized by keeping a digital backup of her medical records and setting up a designated space for medication and related documents. Having everything in one place made it easier for her and her family to focus on her recovery rather than scrambling for information. Then there's the Brandon family, who weathered a natural disaster gracefully by having a detailed emergency plan. Their pre-packed emergency kits and clear communication plan kept them calm and collected when the storm hit. And let's not forget about Mark, a professional who adapted his organizational strategies after losing his job. By reaching out to his network for support and using digital tools to manage job applications and interviews, he navigated the challenging transition with confidence.

Though crises are never welcome, they can be managed with a dash of preparation and flexibility. Embrace life's unpredictability as a chance to refine your organizational skills and build resilience. In the final chapter, we'll delve into cultivating a long-term, organized life, where the lessons learned during crises can be integrated into everyday practices, helping you create a more intentional and fulfilling life.

12
CULTIVATING A LONG-TERM ORGANIZED LIFE

Imagine walking into your home and being greeted with calm and order. The shoes are neatly lined up by the door, the kitchen is clutter-free, and your living room feels like a sanctuary, not a storage unit. It's a scene from a magazine, yet it's your reality. Achieving this level of organization isn't just about tidying up; it's about reflecting on your progress and celebrating each step. Let's explore how reflection can reinforce positive habits and motivate you on your journey to a more organized life.

Reflection is a powerful tool in maintaining organization. It's like having a personal GPS that recalibrates your route based on where you've been and where you want to go. When you take the time to look back on your accomplishments, you reinforce positive behaviors. You see patterns in what works well and identify areas needing tweaking. Acknowledging your achievements provides a psychological boost, much like the satisfaction of crossing a finish line. It releases feel-good chemicals in your brain, boosting your motivation to keep going.

Reflecting on your organizational journey is more than a mental exercise; it's an opportunity to document your milestones and successes. Keeping a journal is a practical way to track your progress. When you clear a closet or organize a drawer, jot it down. Write about how it made you feel and what you learned. Setting aside time monthly or quarterly for reflection can help you assess your progress. It's like a mini-review session, where you can celebrate victories and recalibrate your approach for the future. Using photos or videos to track changes visually can be incredibly rewarding. Imagine flipping through a digital album of your home's transformation—it's like a highlight reel of your hard work.

Celebrating your achievements is just as important as the reflection itself. It's about acknowledging the effort you've put in and rewarding yourself for it. Treat yourself to something special when you hit an organizational milestone. It doesn't have to be extravagant; perhaps a favorite meal or a quiet afternoon with a book. Share your successes with friends and family—they'll be your cheerleaders, celebrating alongside you. Creating a visual representation of your progress, like a scrapbook or digital album, can also be motivating. It's a tangible reminder of how far you've come and the changes you've made.

Take Claire, for instance. She started her organizational journey with a cluttered attic that looked more like a scene from a hoarder's reality show. By keeping a journal, she tracked her progress, from sorting through old boxes to redesigning the space. Her journal entries became a source of motivation, reminding her of what she'd accomplished. Claire celebrated her achievements by hosting a small gathering in her newly organized attic, sharing her success with friends who cheered her on.

Then there's the Haines family, who decided to tackle their chaotic garage. They set small goals and celebrated each milestone with a family pizza night. Over time, they transformed the garage into a functional space with a workstation and organized storage. The celebrations kept them motivated, and they created a photo album to document their progress. It now serves as a reminder of their teamwork and perseverance.

Lastly, I met Graham, a professional who struggled with a messy home office. He took photos of his workspace before and after each organizational session. These images became a powerful visual aid, showcasing the transformation of his environment. Graham shared these photos with his colleagues, inspiring them to start their organizational projects. His journey didn't just improve his work-life balance—it sparked a wave of change among his peers.

Interactive Element: Reflection Exercise

Set aside 15 minutes each month to reflect on your organizational progress. In a journal, write about the tasks you've completed and the emotions tied to them. Include photos or sketches if you like. Review your entries quarterly to celebrate your achievements and adjust your goals. Share your reflections with a friend or family member to invite support and encouragement.

CONTINUOUS IMPROVEMENT: ALWAYS FINDING BETTER WAYS

Picture yourself as an experimental chef in your kitchen, constantly tweaking the recipe to perfection. That's the essence of continuous improvement. It's about regularly stirring the pot, adding a pinch of this or a dash of that, to find the perfect blend that suits your lifestyle. This ongoing refinement and adaptation can lead to a sustained sense of organization and growth. You see, regularly evaluating and adjusting your systems is like giving your home a mini-makeover whenever it feels a bit stale. It keeps things fresh and functional, creating an environment that can better withstand life's inevitable curveballs.

Continuous improvement is your secret ingredient for resilience and adaptability. It helps you bounce back from setbacks, much like a plant that thrives with just the right amount of water and sunlight. You're better equipped to handle whatever life throws your way by continually assessing your organizational strategies. Regular reviews of your routines and systems are vital. Pencil in time each month—not just to declutter, but to critically assess how well your current systems work. Are your storage solutions as efficient as they could be? Is your morning routine helping you start the day on a high note, or does it need a little tweak?

Feedback is a gift, even if it comes from your housemates who are less than thrilled with the current state of the shared bathroom. Encourage open dialogues about what's working and what isn't. Sometimes, an outsider's perspective can reveal blind spots you hadn't noticed. Staying informed about new organizational tools and techniques can also supercharge your efforts. In a world where innovation is just a click away, finding solutions that fit your unique needs is easier than ever. Whether it's a new app for task management or a novel storage solution, keeping abreast of the latest trends can inspire improvements you hadn't considered.

A growth mindset is your best ally in this process. Instead of seeing challenges as roadblocks, view them as stepping stones. Embrace change with open arms and be willing to try new ideas, even if they initially sound a bit odd. Set new goals and challenges to keep your organizational journey interesting. Remember, learning from setbacks is not just about bouncing back—it's about bouncing forward. Use any missteps as motivation to find better ways of doing things. It's like learning to ride a bike; each wobble is part of finding balance.

Take, for instance, Diane, who found herself regularly wrestling with a chaotic home office. By setting aside time each month to review her setup, she gradually refined her workspace to better suit her needs. She discovered that a simple change—adding a whiteboard for daily tasks—drastically improved her productivity. Then there's the Martin family, who adapted their routines as their children grew. What worked for toddlers no longer suited their busy teenagers, so they updated their systems to accommodate new schedules and responsibilities. This adaptability kept their home running smoothly despite the chaos of family life.

Let's not forget about Jake, a reader who dived into the world of organizational tools and techniques. He became a veritable connoisseur of apps and gadgets, testing everything from digital calendars to smart storage solutions. Each discovery brought excitement and possibility, pushing him to update and improve his organizational systems continually. Jake's enthusiasm for experimentation ensured that his home and life remained organized but also vibrant and dynamic.

EMBRACING MINIMALISM: SIMPLIFYING TO INCREASE JOY

What if your home transformed into a tranquil haven where each item has a purpose, and clutter is a thing of the past? This is the promise of minimalism. It's not just about having fewer things; it's about enhancing your life by focusing on quality over quantity. Imagine walking into your living room and seeing only the essentials—an inviting sofa, a lamp that casts a warm glow, and a single cherished piece of art on the wall. The benefits of reducing clutter extend beyond aesthetic appeal. Simplifying your surroundings can lead to a profound sense of well-being. It reduces the mental load of managing endless possessions, allowing you to focus on what truly matters. You'll find that your home becomes a reflection of your inner peace, offering a respite from the chaos of the outside world.

Embracing minimalism requires a shift in mindset. Start by conducting regular decluttering sessions. These aren't just cleaning frenzies; they're opportunities to evaluate what adds value to your life. As you sort through your belongings, ask yourself if each item serves a purpose or brings joy. If it doesn't, it might be time to let it go. Prioritizing experiences

CULTIVATING A LONG-TERM ORGANIZED LIFE • 131

and relationships over material goods is another cornerstone of minimalism. Instead of buying more stuff, invest in creating memories with loved ones. Whether it's a weekend getaway or a simple dinner at home, these moments will enrich your life far more than any gadget ever could. Practicing mindful consumption is key. Before making a purchase, consider whether it's something you truly need or just a fleeting desire.

The concept of "enough" is central to minimalism. It's about finding contentment with what you have rather than constantly chasing more. Set limits on your possessions and stick to them. This doesn't mean living a spartan life devoid of beauty; it means curating your belongings to reflect your values. Discover the joy in simplicity and sufficiency. A wardrobe with fewer clothes can make getting dressed a breeze. A kitchen with only the essentials can turn cooking into a delightful experience. Avoiding the trap of consumerism and the pursuit of excess frees you from the endless cycle of wanting more. It's liberating to realize that happiness doesn't come from accumulating things but from appreciating what you already have.

I remember Jackie, a reader who downsized her home after her children moved out. Letting go of decades of accumulated stuff was daunting, but it led to a greater sense of happiness. Her smaller home became a sanctuary filled only with items she loved. Then there's the Norbert family, who decided to simplify their living space after feeling overwhelmed by clutter. They focused on creating a home that supported their lifestyle, with open spaces for their children to play and areas dedicated to family activities. This shift improved their quality of life, reducing stress and fostering stronger connections. Finally, meet Alex, a busy professional who adopted minimalism to reduce stress and increase focus. He found that his mind was clearer by eliminating distractions, and his productivity soared. His minimalist workspace, free from unnecessary items, became a place where creativity flourished.

CREATING YOUR IDEAL LIFE: LIVING WITH INTENTION AND PURPOSE

Living with intention is like steering your own ship, charting a course that aligns with your values and aspirations. It's about waking up daily with a clear sense of purpose, knowing that your actions are not just random motions but deliberate steps toward a meaningful destination. This approach to life can do wonders for your well-being, bringing a sense of fulfillment and joy. When you align your daily actions with your long-term goals and core values, you're not just going through the motions; you're living with purpose. This alignment fosters a sense of direction and meaning, like finding the true north on your compass.

To cultivate a lifestyle filled with intention and purpose, set clear, meaningful goals. These goals act as signposts, guiding your path and keeping you on track. Regularly reviewing these goals ensures you're moving in the right direction, adjusting as needed. Creating a vision board can be a powerful tool in this process. It's a visual representation of your dreams and aspirations, constantly reminding you of what you're working towards. When you see your goals displayed visually, they're no longer just abstract ideas; they become tangible targets you can aim for.

Mindfulness and self-reflection are crucial practices in this journey. They help you stay connected to your values, ensuring your actions align with your true self. Take time each day to reflect on your choices and consider whether they move you closer to your ideal life. This introspection doesn't have to be an elaborate ritual. It can be as simple as a few quiet moments with your morning coffee, contemplating the day ahead and the steps you'll take to live with intention.

Designing your ideal life involves identifying and prioritizing your core values and passions. What truly matters to you? What brings you joy and fulfillment? These questions are the foundation upon which you'll build your life. Simplifying your daily routines can also help you focus on what truly matters. By eliminating unnecessary tasks and distractions, you create space for the things that align with your values. Building habits that support your long-term goals and well-being is another key strategy. These habits become the building blocks of your ideal life, reinforcing your commitment to living with purpose.

Consider the story of Emma, who found herself unfulfilled in her corporate job. She realized her passion lay in helping others, so she aligned her career with her values by transitioning to a role in social work. This change brought her a deep sense of satisfaction and purpose as she finally did work that resonated with her soul. Then there's the Morecambe family, who created a home environment reflecting their values. They prioritized family time and created spaces that encouraged togetherness and connection. This shift strengthened their bond and brought a sense of harmony to their household.

Finally, meet David, a reader who adopted habits to support his long-term well-being. He identified his passion for health and fitness and integrated it into his daily routine. By prioritizing his workouts and making time for meal prep, he created a lifestyle that supported his physical health and brought him immense joy.

Creating your ideal life is deeply personal, and there's no one-size-fits-all approach. It's about finding what works for you, what brings you joy, and what aligns with your values. As you continue to explore these ideas, remember that living with intention is not about achieving perfection. It's about making deliberate choices that bring you closer to the life you want to live. As we wrap up this chapter, consider how you can apply these principles to your own life, crafting a path that reflects your unique aspirations and desires. This chapter sets the stage for exploring how to maintain these practices long-term, ensuring that your ideal life remains an achievable, sustainable reality.

CONCLUSION

So here we are, at the finish line of our journey together. Can you believe how far you've come? This book set out to be your trusty sidekick in navigating the whirlwind world of ADHD and organization. The goal was to transform that daily chaos into a calm, organized life where stress takes a backseat, and you can truly enjoy the ride.

Throughout these chapters, we've explored the intricate workings of the ADHD brain and the challenges you face with executive dysfunction, disorganization, and emotional overwhelm. We've tackled decluttering, time management, and setting realistic goals. We've even ventured into personal spaces, digital realms, and the importance of involving family and friends in your organizational quest. Each section offers strategies and insights designed to make life a bit easier and more intentional.

But let's be real. Life isn't all about checklists and schedules. It's about finding what works for you, celebrating small victories, and learning to dance with the occasional mess.

Whatever your unique challenges, remember you have the power to create a life that reflects your values and aspirations. Whether it's through embracing minimalism, mastering time management, or simply finding your "why," the tools are now at your disposal.

Now, I invite you to take action. Choose one strategy that resonates with you and implement it. Maybe it's setting up a morning routine or tackling that cluttered closet. Perhaps it's starting a mindfulness practice or embracing the Pomodoro Technique for better focus. Whatever it is, take that first step and see where it leads you. Remember, progress is progress, no matter how small.

And hey, don't forget to celebrate your achievements along the way! Every step you take towards a more organized life is worth acknowledging. Treat yourself to a little reward, share your successes with loved ones, and reflect on how far you've come. These moments of celebration reinforce your efforts and motivate you to keep going.

As you continue this journey, embrace the ups and downs with humor and grace. Organization isn't about perfection; it's about creating a life that feels good. Be kind to yourself when things get messy, and remember that each new day offers a fresh start. You have the strength and resilience to overcome obstacles and craft a life that aligns with your true self.

So, here's a little affirmation to carry with you: "I am capable of creating a life that reflects my values and brings me joy. My journey is unique, and I embrace it with confidence and grace."

Thank you for allowing me to guide you through this journey. Your willingness to explore, learn, and grow is truly inspiring. You're not just organizing your physical space; you're creating a life filled with intention and purpose. Keep this book close, refer to it whenever you need a boost, and remember that you've got this.

Here's to a future filled with clarity, calm, and the freedom to live your best life. Cheers to you and the incredible journey ahead!

REFERENCES

Executive Dysfunction: What It Is, Symptoms & Treatment https://my.clevelandclinic.org/health/symptoms/23224-executive-dysfunction#:

Functional Roles of Norepinephrine and Dopamine in ADHD https://www.medscape.org/viewarticle/523887

9 Tips for Creating a Routine for Adults with ADHD https://psychcentral.com/adhd/9-tips-for-creating-a-routine-for-adults-with-adhd

Managing Disorganization in ADHD https://www.verywellmind.com/how-to-recognize-and-manage-disorganization-in-adhd-5216668

How to Create SMART Decluttering Action Plan to Get ... https://www.saturdaygift.com/how-to-create-smart-decluttering-action-plan/

Why Getting Organized is Good for Your Mental Health https://alliancehealthequity.org/why-getting-organized-is-good-for-your-mental-health/

ADHD and Fear of Failure https://focusedmindadhdcounseling.com/adhd-and-fear-of-failure/

50 Quick Wins for Decluttering Your House | Adrian's Crazy Life https://adrianscrazylife.com/50-quick-wins-for-decluttering/

Pomodoro Technique for ADHD: Why it Helps & How ... https://www.choosingtherapy.com/pomodoro-technique-adhd/

Mastering Time Blocking for ADHD: Your Ultimate Guide to ... https://dayoptimizer.com/adhd/mastering-time-blocking-for-adhd-your-ultimate-guide-to-better-focus/

Eisenhower Matrix: Decision-Making Tool for ADHD Adults https://www.additudemag.com/download/eisenhower-matrix-adhd-prioritization/

How to Manage Procrastination if You Have ADHD https://www.healthline.com/health/adhd/adhd-procrastination

Small Entryway Storage Ideas to Meet All Your Drop Zone ... https://www.bhg.com/decorating/storage/mudroom/smart-storage-for-small-entryways/

Kitchen Organizing Tips for Cluttered Adults with ADHD https://www.additudemag.com/slideshows/kitchen-organizing-tips-for-adhd/

The Ultimate Living Room Decluttering List https://www.southernmotion.com/blog/2020/05/ultimate-living-room-decluttering-list/

REFERENCES

How to Declutter and Organize Your Bedroom for Better ... https://www.sleep.com/sleep-health/organize-bedroom

6 BENEFITS TO HAVING AN ORGANIZED CLOSET https://www.linkedin.com/pulse/6-benefits-having-organized-closet-bymarydyann

How to Declutter Your Closet: A Step-by-Step Guide https://www.coverstore.com/blog/post/how-to-declutter-closet-a-step-by-step-guide

43 Small Bathroom Storage Ideas, Plus Organizing Tips https://www.thespruce.com/very-small-bathroom-storage-ideas-5324097

How to Get Organized with Adult ADHD https://www.additudemag.com/how-to-get-organized-with-adhd/

Inbox Zero: Secrets and Tricks - Keeping https://www.keeping.com/content/inbox-zero/

Best 13 Email management software of 2024 https://www.zendesk.com/service/ticketing-system/email-management-software/

How to Organize Your Digital Files | Reviews by Wirecutter https://www.nytimes.com/wirecutter/guides/how-to-organize-your-digital-files/

Top 10 Apps Redefining The Digital Detox https://techround.co.uk/startups/top-10-startups-digital-detox/

9 Tips for Creating a Routine for Adults with ADHD https://psychcentral.com/adhd/9-tips-for-creating-a-routine-for-adults-with-adhd

How to Build New Habits by Taking Advantage of Old Ones https://jamesclear.com/habit-stacking#:

The Ultimate House Maintenance Checklist for Homeowners https://www.abt.com/learn/the-ultimate-house-maintenance-checklist-for-homeowners

How Adults with ADHD Can "Manufacture" Motivation https://www.psychologytoday.com/us/blog/rethinking-adult-adhd/202103/how-adults-adhd-can-manufacture-motivation

How to Declutter Your Home with Mindfulness https://clutterfreenow.com/how-to-declutter-your-home-with-mindfulness/

How Clutter Can Affect Your Health https://www.webmd.com/balance/ss/slideshow-clutter-affects-health

7 Decluttering Tips: How to Release Your Attachment ... https://tinybuddha.com/blog/7-decluttering-tips-release-attachment-stuff/

Decluttering Affirmations to Help You Transform Your ... https://medium.com/the-decluttered-soul/decluttering-affirmations-to-help-you-transform-your-home-and-the-way-you-think-about-clutter-2c0cd4bc376b

ADHD: The Strength of a Checklist | Psychology Today https://www.psychologytoday.com/us/blog/balanced/202302/adhd-the-strength-of-a-checklist#:

REFERENCES

Best Planner Apps For ADHD: How To Increase Motivation ... https://britetodo.com/article/Best-planner-apps-for-ADHD%3A-how-to-increase-motivation-with-ADHD-Planner

The Best Apps For ADHD In 2024: A Guide https://www.forbes.com/health/mind/apps-for-adhd/

ADDA Virtual Peer Support Groups for Adults with ADHD https://add.org/adda-virtual-programs/

Unveiling Effective ADHD Communication Strategies https://justmind.org/adhd-communication-strategies/

How to Involve Your Family in the Organizing Process https://www.simplifiedspacesorganizing.com/how-to-involve-your-family-in-the-organizing-process-tips-for-a-team-effort

Organizational skills training for children with ADHD https://www.ncbi.nlm.nih.gov/pmc/articles/PMC8556963/

Conflict Resolution for Parents of ADHD Kids https://www.additudemag.com/family-communication-strategies-adhd-conflict-resolution/

30 Small Apartment Storage Ideas to Maximize Space https://www.thespruce.com/small-apartment-storage-ideas-7369679

Moving Checklist: Ultimate Guide to an Organized Move https://getorganizedhq.com/moving-checklist/

Declutter and Organize for the Holidays in 6 Steps https://www.dumpsters.com/blog/organizing-for-the-holidays

How To Successfully Cope With Unexpected Events & Stay ... https://dnqsolutions.com/how-to-successfully-cope-with-unexpected-events-stay-organized/

ADHD and Metacognition: Learning to reflect on your thoughts ... https://drsharonsaline.com/2021/10/25/adhd-and-metacognition-learning-to-reflect-on-your-thoughts-and-experiences-with-a-growth-mindset/#:

Minimalism and ADHD (Attention Deficit Hyperactivity ... https://balancethroughsimplicity.com/minimalism-and-adhd/

32 of the Best Ways to Get Organized When You Have ADHD https://psychcentral.com/adhd/the-best-ways-to-get-organized-when-you-have-adhd

Intention Deficit Disorder: Why ADHD Minds Can't Turn ... https://www.additudemag.com/intention-deficit-disorder-adhd/

Printed in Dunstable, United Kingdom